TWENTY WAYS
TO IMPROVE
CUSTOMER SERVICE

Lloyd C. Finch

Crisp Publications

Twenty Ways to Improve Customer Service

Lloyd C. Finch

CREDITS

Editor: Follin Armfield
Typesetter: Execustaff
Illustrations: Kurt Hanks
Cover Design: Kathleen Barcos

Copyright © 1994 by Crisp Publications, Inc.
Printed in the United States of America

English language Crisp books are distributed worldwide. Our major international distributors include:

CANADA: Reid Publishing Ltd., Box 69559—109 Thomas St., Oakville, Ontario, Canada L6J 7R4. TEL: (905) 842-4428, FAX: (905) 842-9327

Raincoast Books Distribution Ltd., 112 East 3rd Avenue, Vancouver, British Columbia, Canada V5T 1C8. TEL: (604) 873-6581, FAX: (604) 874-2711

AUSTRALIA: Career Builders, P.O. Box 1051, Springwood, Brisbane, Queensland, Australia 4127. TEL: 841-1061, FAX: 841-1580

NEW ZEALAND: Career Builders, P.O. Box 571, Manurewa, Auckland, New Zealand. TEL: 266-5276, FAX: 266-4152

JAPAN: Phoenix Associates Co., Mizuho Bldg. 2-12-2, Kami Osaki, Shinagawa-Ku, Tokyo 141, Japan. TEL: 3-443-7231, FAX: 3-443-7640

Selected Crisp titles are also available in other languages. Contact International Rights Manager Suzanne Kelly at (415) 323-6100 for more information.

Library of Congress Catalog Card Number 93-073184
Finch, Lloyd
Twenty Ways to Improve Customer Service
ISBN 1-56052-246-1

dedicated to
Vivyan Ann Finch

About the Author

Lloyd Finch is President of Alpha Consulting Group, a company devoted to customer service training and the development of service improvement programs. The organization also produces training videos designed for service and sales employees. Lloyd is an experienced speaker on customer service issues. Prior to forming

Alpha Consulting he had extensive marketing, sales, and customer service experience in an 18 year career as a manager with Pacific Bell and AT&T.

Other Books by the Author
Telephone Courtesy and Customer Service, Crisp Publications, Inc.

Contents

Introduction

This Book, the Customer Service Situation, Your Job and Opportunity

This book is for those interested in improving customer service, especially for those who provide frontline customer service. The book presents ideas, skills, suggestions and recommended personal actions to help service providers increase their personal skill inventory. Each person involved with customers has an inventory of skills. A situation arises and, to satisfy the customer, we reach into our mental inventory and bring up what is needed. We might draw upon an existing skill or idea, or create a solution to a customer problem. The more powerful and well stocked our mental inventory, the stronger the service performance.

A Great Opportunity

The current customer service situation offers a great opportunity to excel, to be the best, to separate your organization and yourself from the pack. Why? Because too many organizations do not measure up to high service standards. They talk quality, but often deliver something less.

This gives you the opportunity to take advantage of the situation. The frontline service provider can step up to quality by providing strong service and, in the process, charge ahead of the competition. How? One way is to add skills that satisfy customers.

Skills and Knowledge

A wise man once wrote, "If you don't know where you're going, any road will take you there." The trick is deciding what you want—successful customer service—and following the shortest road there. It can be an enjoyable and rewarding one to travel. It is also an ongoing learning experience.

Look around your organization at the people you work with. Identify the top performers. Spotlight these top-notch people and see what they have in common. You will typically find two things:

- **A large inventory of skills**

- **A constant search for new skills and knowledge**

Your Service Level

In training for customer service, the instructor often asks the group to rate the service they provide by using a 1 to 10 scale. One is poor, 5 is average and, of course, 10 is excellent service. The ratings typically fall above average, around 6 or 7. Once the ratings have been expressed, the instructor begins a discussion by asking, "How can you improve?" There are two standard replies. First: "I need added skill in dealing with customers." Second: "I need more knowledge." From this training observation, we can conclude that the important factors in improving customer service are:

- **Additional skills**

- **Increased knowledge**

- **Experience**

Increased knowledge refers to overall job knowledge. This includes all the information required to discuss and present products or services thoroughly.

How do you rate *your* service? To improve that rating, what do you need to do? As a frontline service provider, how good do you want to be? If your goal is not completely clear, allow a suggestion: **Strive to be a professional in every aspect of your job. Be a 10.** It will require commitment, greater knowledge about your job and added skill in delivering service to customers. This includes telephone and face-to-face skills for both external and internal customers.

Quality

Quality has become the most sought-after part of the customer service success formula. Here are two examples.

Hamburgers, Fries, Salads and Tacos

Do you like fast food? You are probably familiar with McDonald's, Burger King, Wendy's, Carl's Jr., Taco Bell, Kentucky Fried Chicken and a host of other successful American enterprises. Fast food is an example of service near the 10 level. (Of course, there are a few exceptions, but the principal fast food chains consistently provide quality service.)

There are many reasons why these fast food giants are successful, but the most significant is that they give their customers what they want. Want a low-priced hamburger or taco? It's yours. Like your order served fast? You've got it. Want fresh ingredients? They have them. Want to stay in your car and take away your food in a bag? They cut holes in the sides of their buildings so you can drive up and do just that. In short, they are knowledgeable about customer needs and respond to them.

FACT: Did you know? McDonald's has 8,700 U.S. locations and has earned more than $12.5 billion in U.S. sales. Burger King is number two with 5,400 U.S. locations and U.S. sales of $5.4 billion. McDonald's also has another 3,600 locations outside the United States. This includes 865 in Japan. Do you think McDonald's and the other successful fast food chains understand customers needs?

Restrooms, Security, Telephone Systems, Coffee and Meeting Rooms

I had the good fortune to organize and conduct customer service training for Intel Corporation, General Site Services (GSS) at its Santa Clara, California location. Intel is the number-one computer-chip manufacturer in the world. GSS supports thousands of internal customers by providing basic services. If there is a leaky faucet on the third floor in building 5, you call GSS. If the telephone doesn't work, call GSS. If you need coffee for your meeting, call GSS. Need an electrician? Call GSS. GSS employees talk with internal customers from clerks and managers to Ph.Ds.

Clearly, GSS was well-organized, but there was one overriding problem: Many customers were frustrated because they had difficulty finding the right person to call within GSS. GSS solved the problem by organizing, staffing and implementing a well-planned centralized group called Action Line. Customers just dialed one number for all services. Action Line was staffed with knowledgeable and well-trained employees who could provide immediate assistance or arrange for service. On an average day the group receives nearly 1,300 calls.

Intel GSS identified and then satisfied an important customer need.

Quality service means satisfying customer needs. This theme is repeated in successful organizations around the world.

Quality Service Is Dynamic

There was a time, not so very long ago, when a set of customer skills could carry an individual throughout most of a career. The reasons? Customers demanded less because their needs were simpler. In addition, there was less competition so customers had fewer choices. Today, as you know, that situation has changed. The competition your organization faces is often global, and the marketplace continues to evolve and change. The customer is more sophisticated and demanding. As a result, customer service skills need constant improvement.

Where Does Quality Begin?

Let quality begin with you, the frontline service provider. As you strive to reach that perfect "10" level, you will encounter obstacles and setbacks, but with commitment and hard work you can gather the skills necessary to reach your objective. When customer after customer is satisfied, you will know you're there.

The following ideas for improving customer service come with a guarantee for the service provider: Implement the ideas and suggestions presented, and your service performance will become even stronger and your customers more satisfied.

Provide Extra Service

Extra service is service that goes beyond the minimum. Too often when a customer calls or comes in for a face-to-face meeting, the inquiry is quickly taken care of. This is good, right? Minimal information is dispensed in the least amount of time. Very efficient, neat and clean! But were the customer's needs satisfied? Maybe! Remember, there is an important difference between just providing an answer and giving a customer extra service.

Extra service adds value to the transaction or the contact. You can be a value-added service provider by offering information and being of greater service. Stated another way, you add value to the customer contact, and the customer receives more benefit.

There are three basic steps that lead to extra service:

1. Before providing service, ask questions to understand thoroughly the customer's inquiry, situation or problem.

2. Determine if there is more service you can offer.

3. Ask if the customer is satisfied.

Step 1. Before Providing Service, Ask Questions

Often, the customer's need is immediately clear. However, when there is the slightest doubt, explore the situation for further understanding before taking action. This will save time and reduce confusion.

A Case in Point
A customer called her cable television company and asked, "Do I have the

Sports Channel?" The representative quickly checked the customer's record and said, "No, you don't have the Sports Channel." The customer's immediate response was; "I need to add it. How much is it?" Suppose you were the cable representative. What would you do next?

Since the customer was unsure whether she had the Sports Channel, the representative thought there might be some confusion over the cable offerings. She decided to use step 1, and replied, "The cost is $8.98 per month, and I'll be glad to order it for you. What prompted your interest?" The customer replied that her family liked to watch college basketball, and according to the newspaper, the games were available only on the Sports Channel. The representative went on to explain the newspaper was wrong and the games were broadcast on an existing channel. The customer did not need the Sports Channel in order to view college basketball.

The representative did a good job of using step 1, trying to understand the customer's inquiry. She understood the inquiry because she uncovered the customer's motivation or reason.

Motivation
Learning the motivation behind a customer question or request is often the key to satisfying needs. This can often be done with a simple question similar to what the cable representative asked. **"What prompted your interest?"** What a great question!

Let's look at five more leading questions you can use that will help unlock customer motivation and pave the way for a thorough understanding of the customer's inquiry.

Five Questions
1. Why did you decide on this particular _____? (fill in the

blank with your words—e.g., product, service, size, arrangement, etc.)

2. How do you plan to use _____? (product, new service, new account, etc.)

3. How do you see this working for you? (referring to systems, products and services)

4. Who in your organization will be using _____? (perhaps a different application or service because of who is using it)

5. What brought this to your attention? (referring to the error, the situation, new information or the "why" behind the request or problem)

Another Situation
In the furniture department of a major store a couple was examining a sofa that had a large "sale" sign on it. They looked interested.

A sales clerk approached and asked, "May I help you?"

The woman spoke first. "Yes. We're interested in this sofa."

The salesperson responded, "It's on sale for $395.00."

The man nodded because the sale sign already told him the price. The woman asked, "How long is it?"

The salesperson replied, "It's six feet." Following a moment or two of silence, the salesperson excused himself and said he would be back in a few moments.

A few minutes later the couple left.

Had our first step been used and the customer's motivation explored, the sofa might now be in the couple's home instead of the store. There was no service, therefore no sale.

What should the salesperson have done? First, the salesperson needed to use step 1 and ask a few questions to determine the customer's needs. He might have begun with one of the recommended leading questions, "How do you plan to use the sofa?" This might have led to a discussion about colors, fabrics, carpet and other furniture in the room. Eventually, the salesperson could help the couple plan the room or maybe the entire house.

By providing this kind of service, the customer receives added value. The customer and the sales or service person form a professional relationship in which they work together in order to find a solution for the customer. Keep in mind, this professional relationship began with a step-1–type question: "How do you plan to use the sofa?"

What About Customer Problems? How Can Value Be Added?

When the customer has a problem, there is often a great opportunity for extra service. The service provider can be of added value to the customer by identifying the problem's cause and offering a solution. When this is done successfully, the customer places considerably more value on the service received. The customer service representative is seen as a resource who helps the customer's business.

Let's look at an example.

The hot air, air conditioning system. On a very hot day the air conditioning in your office blows out only warm air. You call a technician, and she is able to get the system operating within a few minutes. The next day is even hotter and again the air conditioning blows warm air. The same technician comes out and gets the system up and running. The next day it happens again. This time you call a different vendor, and the technician who looks at the problem concludes it is caused by a faulty thermostat. She installs a new thermostat and then, using step 1, asks a few questions about the use of the air conditioning system. She shows you a typical cost savings brought about by a low-cost maintenance schedule. To avoid future problems and to save you money, she recommends the maintenance schedule. You purchase the maintenance plan.

The second technician solved the problem by eliminating the cause. She provided extra service and became a value-added resource to your organization.

Step 2. Determine If There Is More Service You Can Offer

Before you conclude the conversation with your customer, ask yourself if there is more service you can offer. Perhaps the customer needs additional information or could use other services.

Remember our furniture store example: The salesperson failed to explore the customer's inquiry and, as a result, missed the opportunity to offer more service. The customers wanted to be offfered more service than just a price quote and a verification of the sofa's length.

Step 3. Ask If the Customer Is Satisfied

Too often we think we're doing such a fine job of satisfying the customer that we fail to ask if we really are. Some service providers are a bit afraid of the customer's opinion and don't want to know what the customer thinks. They are members of the **"No-news-is-good-news club."** At their meetings they

3

say things to each other such as, "The customer never complains, so everything must be okay." Or, "I can't imagine why there would be a problem." Or, "Our service was excellent, but that ungrateful customer left us anyway."

Knowing what customers think about your service is always important. When they are satisfied, what you are doing is correct. And if they are unhappy, you can fix it. The following survey results tell us customers generally don't complain, they just go away.

A Customer Study About Satisfaction

The Research Institute of America reports that the White House Office of Consumer Affairs determined these findings, based on a 1985 study:

- 96 percent of unhappy customers never complain about rude treatment.

- At least 90 percent who are dissatisfied with the service they received will not buy again or come back.

- To make matters worse, these dissatisfied customers will tell their story to at least nine other people.

- 13 percent will tell their unhappy story to 20 other people.

You **must** minimize unhappy customers. So occasionally ask your customer, "How satisfied are you with our service? How can we improve our service to you?" Some customer service providers feel they are excused from asking because their organization already conducts customer surveys. Wrong! Ask. Find out. Be a professional.

When You Ask, Be Prepared for the Answer

There is always a risk when you ask customers if they are satisfied. The response will be either positive ("Where's the boss? She needs to hear this.") or negative ("Why did I ask?"). When it's positive, it can be fun. The customer praises the respresentative and points out what a great organization he works for. It gives a little lift to the service provider's day. He instantly feels better about nearly everything.

On the other hand, a negative response can leave you with the opposite feeling. It takes courage to ask if the customer is satisfied, but it must be done if quality is the goal.

What to Do with the Response

When the customer praises your organization, it's important to share the good news with other team members. Let all who participated know they made an important contribution.

When the response is negative, you have a problem—a dissatisfied customer. This customer deserves a response, one that immediately addresses the situation and/or offers a plan to avoid a recurrence. Not responding only adds to the customer's unhappy state.

A basic "nonresponse" example.

Many restaurant cashiers are instructed to ask the customer how their meal was. In the average situation the cashier does not seem to be prepared for a negative response. The customer says the meal was marginal or worse, and the cashier is suddenly tongue-tied. The cashier is probably not empowered to do much about the situation and normally not trained in customer service.

The restaurant situation is a basic example of making a negative customer service situation even worse. The worst offense of all is not to respond appropriately to a dissatisfied customer. The response you offer depends on the severity of the situation. Obviously, action needs to be taken to correct the problem, or at a minimum an apology may be in order. When appropriate, develop a plan to prevent the same thing from happening in the future.

Let the customer know. When there is an action plan, it's important to make the customer aware of what has been done to correct the negative situation. However, there are times and particular customers where everything may best be left unsaid. Therefore, it's a good idea to ask, "We've taken care of the situation that caused you so many problems. Would you like to hear the details?" Keep in mind not to share confidential information or anything that would embarrass your organization.

Let's Talk about Price and Extra Service

As we discussed, adding extra service and providing value-added service are two important keys to customer service success. But how does price fit in with being a value-added service provider? In other words, if the customer bases a purchase on price, how can you provide value-added service?

Let's talk about the service job. It usually falls into one of two general categories.

The first category is where services are the main feature. Since we're all familiar with banks, let's use their services of savings, checking and loans to illustrate the point. Customer-contact employees at banks provide customer service around these and other services.

The second type of service job is where a product is ordered or sold and customer service is provided around the order and in support of the product. Shopping in your favorite retail store or ordering over the telephone using a catalog or product list are good examples. System sales support is another example.

Both situations offer considerable room to provide the value-added extra service that will distinguish you from your competitors. But many customer service providers believe their customers make decisions only on price. Sometimes this is true, but only when service employees and salespeople fail to distinguish their products or services, and thus leave the customer with no choice but to place price first.

Commodity products. Author Mack Hanan, in his book *System Selling Strategies*, describes the "price-first" situation well. He states, "When customers perceive a product as too expensive or no better than that of the competition, the product is being classified as a commodity." Hanan goes on to say, "Since the only point of difference between utilities is usually the price, customers bargain with suppliers to drive price down as close as possible to cost."

Avoid the price trap. It's common for frontline people to put themselves in this "price" position unnecessarily. It can usually be avoided with constant emphasis on other benefits and the use of added-value service. If you believe all you have is price, soon someone will beat you with a lower price. You must offer service, not be just someone who quotes prices.

How to get away from price. The customer asks, "What does it cost?" In reply, state the price and, when appropriate, immediately talk about services and benefits associated with the product or service. Customers are generally interested in more than price. They want support, service, advice, help, fast response, to save money and time, professionalism, accuracy, someone who will listen, reliability and much more. Provide these wants and needs, and price will diminish in importance.

A Conclusion

Let's close this first chapter with a final thought about extra service. Providing extra service on a consistent basis will lead to the customer's perceiving the service as a value added and the representative as an added resource who helps the customer's business. When a service provider achieves this status with a customer, it is a summit. The air is a little rarefied, but the service person is now among the few who are the very best. It is worth striving for.

Case Study: The Distribution Company

The American Distribution Company carried a wide range of products. Its priority, like other companies in its industry, was asset management and sales/service. Most of the salespeople and customer service representatives (CSRs) spent the better part of their business day on the telephone discussing products with customers. The competition within most of American Distribution's product lines was intense. As a result, price played a big role in the customer's decision. Unfortunately, some American Distribution salespeople and CSRs thought price was so important that this was often all they discussed with customers. These CSRs and salespeople recognized the competitive position they were in and responded to it by becoming primarily price quoters rather than service providers. The company gave their representatives considerable latitude in determining product gross margin within certain guidelines. The result was an advantage for the CSRs because they could negotiate price when necessary. The disadvantage was that products were often sold at a lower cost than necessary.

Mike the CSR
Mike was a CSR who seemed never to be able to get away from price. He seldom

talked about the benefits his organization offered, which included an enormous inventory capacity and short delivery intervals. Instead, he was first and foremost a price quoter. His conversations often went like this:

Mike: What have you been paying?

Customer: We are currently paying about $22.00 per unit.

Instead of exploring or developing the situation (using the three steps) Mike saw a quick sale opportunity and immediately quoted his lowest price.

Mike: I can beat that price. How does $20.00 per unit sound?

The customer liked the price and placed an order.

What Happened
Let's take a moment to examine what Mike did. First, he got an order, and that's always good news. But in this case there is also some bad news. Mike established himself with the customer as someone who quotes prices and made no attempt to present himself as an added-value resource. He never mentioned the capacity and service of American Distribution or other benefits of doing business with the organization. Mike only offered the customer a price that beat his competition. Therefore, the customer viewed Mike as a seller of commodities—goods that are sold on price only. With this approach, Mike will have difficulty when he is the one with the higher price or perhaps even when price is the same. The next time the customer wants a price quote, he may call Mike. When he wants price and service, we don't know who he might call.

What Could Have Happened
Let's be realistic. Not every situation can be developed into the customer perceiving

added value. This may be especially true in the distribution industry, where so many companies with identical products are competing. However, many situations can be turned away from price, and it is worth the effort to try to influence the customer's perception and attempt to build a long-term relationship. The following dialogue is an example of how Mike's customer conversation might have gone.

Mike: Which product are you currently using?

Customer: The Unitext 2000.

Mike: We have had success with the 2000. It's proved to be very reliable, and I don't believe we have had one returned. By the way, are you familiar with American Distributing?

Customer: I know your name, but that's about all.

Mike: We've been in business for almost 30 years, and we're financially sound. Our customers have found our delivery to be fast because we have three warehouses in the state and can fill your order from any one of them. Have you experienced many order delays?

Customer: Just one or two, but even that can be a problem.

Mike: I know. Our inventory of major manufacturers is very large. For example, while we were talking I checked our inventory level of Unitext 2000s. We have more than 200 in stock. How many were you thinking of ordering?

Customer: We need 20 now and will need another 15 in a month or so.

Mike: What I can do is price the 2000s based on an order of 35 and deliver 20 now and another 15 in a month.

Customer: Will that be two invoices or one?

Mike: Which do you prefer?

Customer: I'd like two invoices. One with each order. Before we go too far let's talk about price. What is your price?

Mike: Let me see what that comes to. What have you been paying?

Customer: $22.00 per unit.

Mike has done a good job of managing the customer conversation up to this point. He stressed the value and benefits of his organization and has made it clear to the customer he has more than price to offer. He also satisfied a customer need by arranging for two invoices. The customer now wants a quote before the order is firm.

What Are You Going to Say Next?
Suppose you were managing this conversation. What would you say to the customer? Remember, as a CSR with American Distributing you have some latitude on the price you quote. For example, let's say you can reduce the price to nineteen dollars and still make a small gross profit for your organization. What are you going to say to the customer? Here are a few choices.

1. "I can meet the $22.00 price. When would you like delivery?"

2. "I can save you a dollar per unit. How does $21.00 sound?"

3. "I can beat that price [$22.00]. I can sell them to you for $19.00 a unit. Will that be all right?"

4. Other?

You can determine what the best customer response is. Of course, we don't know exactly what the customer is thinking. Is she still price sensitive? Probably so. Does she now have more appreciation for the capability and service of American Distribution? Hopefully, yes. Were her needs met regarding the two invoices? Yes. Would she order from Mike at $23.00 per unit? Unlikely. Will she pay $22.00 or $21.00? She probably will. Does she think of Mike as a price quoter or as a value-added resource? Perhaps a little of both.

Here's the Point

In our example, price never went away. It usually doesn't. However, Mike reduced its importance and emphasized the added value of doing business with his organization. As you know, trying to add value doesn't always work. But it works enough of the time to make it worthwhile to try to introduce it in every customer situation.

Be Culturally Aware

Today, customers come from diverse backgrounds—backgrounds composed of many different languages and cultures. English is often spoken as a second or even a third language. Communicating effectively with these customers requires new skills and understanding.

THREE FACTS

1. When the customer and service provider are from the same culture (e.g., American) and speak a common primary language (e.g., English) communicating and satisfying the customer can sometimes be difficult.

2. When the customer and service provider are from different cultures and speak different native languages, communicating and satisfying the customer can be *very* difficult.

3. Many customer service providers fail to show understanding or sensitivity to the customer's culture. Nor do they respond properly to the fact that the customer speaks English as a second language. Communication problems often result.

The next time you are out shopping, watch as store clerks and other service or sales employees encounter diverse customers.

Occasionally, you will witness excellent service, but far too often the service provided is poor because the employee demonstrates a lack of sensitivity to the customer's culture.

Recognize the Difference

As a service provider you can recognize the cultural and language differences among your customers and respond in a positive way. The following information will help toward that goal.

Culture and Language Are Not the Same Thing

It's important to know the difference between culture and language.

Culture: Socially transmitted behavior patterns, arts, beliefs and all other products of human work and thought of a particular community or population.

Language: A system of words formed from combinations and patterns indigenous to people of a particular nation or by a group of people with a shared history or set of traditions.

What Does This Mean?
It tells us that language and culture are different. Therefore, when dealing with a customer from a different culture who speaks English as a second language, communication problems can be caused by language, by culture, or by both.

Language Problem

Here's an illustration of a language problem. In America we have an expression: "It's six of one and a half-dozen of another." This means we view two situations the same; it doesn't make a difference which one we choose.

This standard American idiom and others like it can easily confuse people who speak English as a second language. A business associate of mine was born in Venezuela, educated in Europe and lived in Canada before moving to America. His English is excellent, but he says, "It took me the longest time to understand the 'six-of-one' expression."

For my colleague and others who speak English as a second language, this expression and others like it present a language problem. When translated from English to the customer's native language, the expression makes no sense.

The Translation Process
During language translation, here's what takes place. Your non-native speaker hears the English words, mentally translates them to his or her native language for understanding, then converts the native language back to English in order to reply in English.

This translation process takes time, and it's easy for everyday English language words to be lost or partially obscured. If everyday language can cause confusion, imagine the bewilderment caused by some of your favorite expressions, jokes, slang and plays on words.

Culture Problem

Often customers of a different culture will recognize the words being spoken but fail to capture all of what is being said because complete understanding requires knowledge of American culture. Here's an example: The customer inquires about a problem. The representative responds, "I can make an end run on this and solve the problem." The customer is confused by the response. The representative has said the problem can be solved by using a short cut. However, to fully understand this reply requires some knowledge of American football. Americans, more so than members of other cultures, commonly use sports phrases and words in their language.

Just Get a Base Hit
I recall a funny sales manager I once worked for saying, "I don't need a homer very often. What I want are base hits."

The sales manager was asking for us to make many smaller sales versus just trying to get a big one. It is very unlikely that someone from another culture, upon hearing this baseball analogy, would have the faintest idea what was intended.

Reducing the Risk

When talking with a customer from another culture who speaks English as a second language it is important to stay with basic language to reduce the risk of poor communications. To help you accomplish this, follow these guidelines:

GUIDELINES

1. **Avoid slang, acronyms, plays on words or expressions that are uniquely American.**

   A few examples: "Close but no cigar." "I'll need your John Hancock on this." "It's a piece of cake." "Don't sweat it." "Garbage in, garbage out." "Let me run it up the flag pole for you."

2. **Also avoid jokes, because they may not be understood. In fact, unless you laugh hard at your own punch line, the diverse customer probably won't know it was a joke. Even then, there is still no guarantee.**

3. **Be patient. Keep in mind the language conversion mentioned earlier—it takes time. Allow time for the customer to convert your English to her native language, convert it back to English and deliver a response.**

4. **Be prepared to repeat yourself.**

   Repeat what you said the first time **exactly**. Do not paraphrase. Why? More than likely the customer has missed only some of what you said, perhaps just a word or two, not all of it. Paraphrasing may sound to the customer like something new is being said.

5. **When the customer is having difficulty understanding, speak more slowly. Often, you hear people raise their voices as if speaking louder will make understanding easier. Speaking slower, not louder, will often solve the problem.**

6. **Monitor for understanding. In face-to-face situations observe the customer's body language for obvious signs of discomfort. On the telephone listen for understanding. Note to what degree the customer is participating in the conversation. If you feel the customer has not understood everything, stop and politely offer to go over it again.**

7. **Do not allow the customer to lose face just because he doesn't understand everything you have said. Politely offer to repeat yourself by blaming the problem on some other factor. Here's an example. "This paperwork can be confusing. Let's go over it again." or "The company (your organization) didn't make this easy for us to understand. Let me go over it again."**

   The idea is not to embarrass or blame the customer. Keep in mind that saving face is very important in many cultures.

8. **Throughout your conversation, show sensitivity and understanding toward the customer. Remind yourself that you are talking with someone from another culture who speaks English as a second language. Follow his or her lead. For example, if he or she is serious and formal, match this behavior.**

Differences

To illustrate further differences between cultures, let's consider two examples of American culture that are not found in most other cultures. The first one is time.

To many cultures Americans appear obsessed with time. In fact, we are clock watchers in comparison to most. Others often find us amusing. Think of all the things we do with time. First of all, we like to save it. Therefore, we manage it and try not to waste it by watching it closely. We get up by it, eat by it, drink our coffee by it, and end our day by going to bed by it. We plan our time, constantly refer to it and even read books about it. We always like to know what time it is and therefore continually ask each other, "What time is it?" In business we like to say, "Time is money." In short, time governs our lives.

Others Are Not as Concerned with Time

When speaking with a customer from another culture, keep in mind he may not be in the same rush you are. He may wish to move slower in order to ensure understanding.

Well, we have spent enough time talking about time. Let's move on and talk about our second example of cultural difference. It won't take long.

Americans Are Sometimes Perceived as Abrupt

Our second example of American culture, appropriately enough, also relates to time. It concerns getting down to business. Americans, unlike most cultures, tend to get down to business pretty fast. Usually, the conversation goes something like this.

Customer Service: Good morning. How may I help you?

The customer explains her request.

Customer Service: There are two ways we can solve this problem. First of all. . . .

It's pretty fast and very direct. Even in a more formal setting during a face-to-face meeting, Americans spend very little time exchanging pleasantries and getting to know each other before they start a business conversation. In many cultures this quick-start approach is often considered rude. In America it's considered correct—a time saver!

There Are Times When Time Should Be Taken

When providing service, the nature and design of the job is to get started quickly in order to satisfy the customer. Although most customers appreciate this approach, some do not. When it's appropriate, slow it down and learn about your diverse customer and let him get to know you. Many cultures place more emphasis on the individual than the organization. A customer who thinks like this will be just as interested in you as she is in your organization. She often wants a personal relationship rather than a superficial one where only casual interest in each other is displayed. Many customers of different cultures are looking for the added-value service we discussed in chapter one, yet they want more of it on the personal relationship side than on the business side.

Success Means Stretching Your Comfort Zone

Each of us functons within a particular comfort zone. When we must adopt and learn new ideas or suggestions, we have to stretch our comfort zone to make room. This is how we grow and add to our knowledge basis.

Growth Means Change

Take the example of your organization the last time you experienced a major change. Perhaps you moved or new people were hired or new skills were required. Or perhaps a different supervisor came on the scene. When the events took place, how did the people around you react and adjust? How did you? Are some employees still adjusting? Do a few seem to refuse to adjust and change? When change occurs we need an attitude that says, "Yes. My comfort zone can be stretched. I can let in new situations, people and skills."

Today There Are New Customers

If you have been a service provider for a few years, you probably have noticed that more customers are from other cultures and speak English as a second language. To work effectively with these customers you will have to stretch your comfort zone. The ideas and techniques presented in this chapter will come into play, but your attitude will be a big factor in your success. If you welcome the different customer and strive to understand her culture and display your best be-of-service attitude, everything will work out well. You must set aside prejudice, stereotypes and misinformation to be successful. The more you learn about other people and their cultures, the more understanding and open you will become.

Conclusion

This subject is vast, and there is more to know than is covered here. If your customers come from diverse backgrounds, read and learn about their culture. The more you know about your customer's culture the easier it will be to provide quality service. Remember, diverse customers are looking for service and understanding and will take their business where they find it.

Case Study: Cathy at American Distributing

With several years of experience, Cathy was considered one of the best CSRs at American Distributing. She was assigned to the large-account desk, where she built strong relationships with her customers. Most of her customers had held their particular jobs for a long time and therefore were very knowledgeable about their jobs. All of these customers spoke English as a primary language. This made Cathy's job a little easier.

Then a change occurred at the Acme Corporation, one of Cathy's accounts. Keshab Joshi became her primary customer contact. Within a short period of time Cathy felt Keshab was incompetent because there were constant communication problems. Cathy was frustrated and went to her supervisor to express her concern.

Cathy's Perception

Cathy's supervisor asked her to list all of the problems she was having with Keshab. Cathy listed five complaints.

1. Keshab speaks broken English and is hard to understand.

2. He doesn't understand the products he is ordering.

3. The changes he has made in the ordering procedures cause Cathy additional work.

4. Keshab is very abrupt and often rude.

5. Cathy is unable to build a relationship with the customer and thinks someone else should handle the account.

Meanwhile, over at Acme: Keshab's Perception

Keshab is equally frustrated with Cathy, and he decides to discuss the situation with his friend Jag, who also comes from India but has worked in American business much longer. Keshab tells Jag the following.

1. Cathy speaks rapidly and is difficult to understand.

2. Keshab wants a better understanding of the products he orders, but Cathy won't take the time to help him.

3. Cathy is not cooperating with the new order procedure, and this causes Keshab more work.

4. Cathy is often rude and at times very abrupt.

5. Keshab is thinking about finding a new organization to do business with, but is concerned it won't look good since Acme has done business with American Distribution for so long.

The Solution

Too often situations like this get resolved in a negative way. Perhaps Keshab finds a new distribution company to handle his orders or Cathy is taken off the account and loses face. Maybe the lack of communication continues for a while and everyone remains frustrated. How would you resolve the situation?

The American-Culture Answer

One American-culture method of resolving the problem might be a meeting between the parties, for Cathy and her supervisor to sit down with Keshab for a face-to-face meeting. The meeting is explained to Keshab as a way to provide better service for his organization. The supervisor recommends they lay out the issues in a direct manner and discuss each one. The supervisor furthers suggests that following the discussion Cathy develop an action plan that will satisfy the customer.

What Would You Do?

If you were Cathy or her supervisor, what would you do? Does the meeting sound like a good one? Maybe the customer has a different idea.

The Customer's Idea on How to Resolve the Problem

Keshab is from India, and his culture is much different from the American one. A meeting with Cathy and her supervisor to confront the issues directly is not something that would be done very often, if ever, in Keshab's culture. Instead of the direct approach, Keshab might prefer Cathy or her supervisor to write a letter— a letter suggesting a solution, but not in too direct a fashion. India's culture would view such an action as appropriate because it would provide time for Keshab to review the letter and think about it before responding. Of course, that response might very well be another letter. In fact, Keshab might never want a meeting to confront the issues directly. Instead, he might believe the whole issue can be resolved by exchanging letters. In India, a meeting would seldom be suggested.

Well, What Do You Think Now?

Do you think Keshab is asking for too much? Do you think writing letters back and forth will be too slow? Keep two things in mind. First, Keshab is the customer, and if he doesn't want a meeting, don't try and force one. Second, in many other cultures the less direct method of resolving the situation is preferred. As was mentioned in this chapter, some find the American culture abrupt and entirely too direct.

How to Use This Example

The next time you are speaking with a customer from another culture who speaks English as a second language, keep the case of Cathy and Keshab in mind. Ask yourself if you are demonstrating sensitivity and understanding toward the customer and his culture.

If you don't know much about the customer's culture, take the time to learn about it. These actions will help you satisfy the customer.

Speak Your Customer's Language

Remember the Objective

The objective of every conversation with a customer is to communicate clearly and effectively. That means using language the customer will understand. In all such conversations, there are three important guidelines to follow:

GUIDELINES

1. Communicate in customer language.

2. Make certain the conversation is two way.

3. Ask questions to get the customer involved and to test for understanding.

Guideline 1. Communicate in Customer Language

All organizations have an internal language. It's loaded with acronyms, slang and technical terms. Depending upon your industry, this language can be very complex and often confusing for your customers.

You learn the internal language of your organization as part of your job. Often customers will become comfortable with your internal language and use it as well as those inside the organization. But most customers don't completely understand it, nor should they. Therefore, it's important to remember to talk to customers in their language, using terms and expressions with which they are familiar.

Technical Language

One problem that often surfaces is the use of technical language with so-called "nontechnical or low-tech customers." In many organizations, frontline service providers spend considerable time learning the technical side of their products and services. Along comes this "low-tech customer." Now the technical language (as well as nontechnical internal language that contains acronyms and expressions the average customer doesn't understand) must be converted and explained.

A perfect example. I saw a great example of this exact situation at a computer systems company in San Jose, California.

Upon leaving a meeting, I noticed a tech-support representative lying on the floor of her cubicle, telephone headset in place, patiently talking to a customer. Why on the floor? It was because the conversation had been going on so long that the representative had decided to rest. I stopped and listened for a few minutes. She was doing a perfect job of explaining, in a step-by-step layman manner, what the customer needed to do to bring his computer system up. Nearly all of the language the representative used was nontechnical. It required more time, but satisfied the customer.

Convert Technical Terms

It may require your best effort, but convert those technical terms, acronyms and expressions into easily understood language. Indeed, the more you know about your products or services the easier it will be.

The Exception

If using technical terms is the only way to describe services or products, then you will have to educate the customer as you proceed. Ask about the customer's depth of knowledge and go slowly while explaining particular terms and concepts that might be confusing. The requirement for customers to understand the technical side of the products or services places the service representative in an advantageous position of helping educate the customer. When appropriate, customers want this advice and counsel and will depend on the service provider and learn to trust her. This situation positions the frontline representative for a close working relationship with the customer. It also enables the sales representative to provide value-added service. Everyone benefits.

A Special Word: Esoteric

Above all, don't be an esoteric service provider. Let's define the word "esoteric."

Esoteric: Intended only for people with special knowledge or interest.

Unfortunately, a few frontline service providers like to display their knowledge in a manner that excludes others. They try to impress customers by purposely using complex terms and language. They think, for some strange reason, if they demonstrate their knowledge in an esoteric manner, they will appear smarter. In fact, the opposite is usually the case.

Guideline 1 Continued: The Sex Thing

Most women have experienced the male service type who esoterically makes an attempt at service. A prime example, women report, is the old-fashioned service manager at a garage. The manager speaks the language of the automobile and, because he has a female customer, he intentionally embellishes the language to the point that she has difficulty understanding. On the surface he is providing service, but in reality he is driving the customer away by undermining trust and creating confusion. In this situation, the service is not only esoteric but also rude.

The Problem

The problems of "rudeness" is not limited to antiquated automobile-service managers. Some men resent the female customer and provide a disservice by treating her poorly. Conversely, some women show their resentment toward male customers in a similar manner. These service providers behave badly toward their opposite-sex customers. They often aren't aware they are doing so; it just comes out. All service employees should ask themselves if they treat the opposite sex with an equal "be-of-service" attitude.

The Self Test

How do you rate when it comes to the opposite-sex customer? Here are a few questions that may give you some added insight to your behavior. Respond to the first six statements with a true or false.

1. I prefer to talk with same-sex customers.

2. I have more problems with opposite-sex customers.

3. Opposite-sex customers are more demanding.

4. I usually have to slow down to talk to opposite-sex customers.

5. I am often forced to be more defensive with opposite-sex customers.

6. From my experience, the opposite-sex customer is more likely to get upset.

7. Overall, who do you find the most difficult? Same-sex customer? Opposite-sex customer? Or do you rate them about the same?

There is not much scientific about the above questions, but your answers will provide a clue to your attitude and service behavior. Ideally the first six statements are "false" responses. The seventh question is an individual matter. However, even if you have substantially more difficulty providing service for the opposite-sex customer it doesn't mean the service is any less. Many people, when confronted with the opposite-sex customer, are not as comfortable as they are in other service situations.

Be Realistic
It's important to be realistic about the service you provide. For example, if your response to the self-test raised some doubt, then it's time to think about your service behavior and attitude toward the opposite sex. During your next opposite-

sex customer conversation, monitor yourself closely to see if you are displaying a negative or less-than-desired attitude. Ask a friend of the opposite sex for input about your attitude toward the other sex.

Guideline 2. Make Certain the Conversation Is Two Way

As you know, a major part of the service job is explaining services and products to customers. Too often this explanation becomes a one-way conversation—a near monologue, a "let-me-tell-you-about-us" verbal attack upon the sensibilities of the customer. Sound a little strong? Let's hope it doesn't apply to you or your organization, but far too often the hapless customer merely asks, "What time is it?" and then learns in great detail how the watch was built.

To get the customer involved, ask questions as the conversation proceeds. Ask about his or her situation, particular needs and opinion. Allow time for the customer to respond and comment on what is being said. When necessary, use the standard open-type questions to get the customer more involved.

Guideline 3. Testing for Understanding

When the subject matter is complex, or possibly confusing, you must test for understanding as the conversation

proceeds. Test by asking questions. Offer a softening statement before you ask your "test" question, such as, "This can be confusing. Do you have any questions at this point?" "I hope I haven't made this too complicated. What questions do you have?"

When the customer conversation concludes, ask yourself, Was my language clear? Did I involve the customer in the conversation? Did I provide choices? Did I listen? Was the communication two way? Keep in mind: the objective of every customer conversation to communicate clearly and effectively.

Conclusion

Speaking the customer's language is a basic of quality service. It must be done. Internal language is fine for the office, but don't involve the customer in it. The customer's needs are satisfied only when there is clear communication.

A Case Study: Scaring the Customer Away

An employee from a large national chain store was explaining to a customer the difference between three VCRs that the store offered. The employee's knowledge was very obvious. Just as obvious was the employee's inability to talk to customers. Her explanation to the customer was highly technical and confusing. The customer left without making a purchase. The employee's performance was unprofessional. VCRs are perplexing enough for most customers; who needs added confusion? The same probably applies to your products and services. When all else fails, keep it simple.

The Absolute Need: Two-Way Conversation

In the VCR example, the customer was not involved, because the salesperson overly emphasized technical language in what turned out to be a one-way presentation. In a two-way communication the customer is involved. Keep in mind that customers want to interact and participate. Let them do it! If the customer's question requires a long explanation on your part, break it up and ask the customer questions as you proceed. Listen to the answers. Provide choices and ask for the customer's ideas and thoughts. Let the customer help with the answers. Don't perform a monologue.

Take Ownership

Taking ownership means personally taking responsibility for a customer's order, problem, inquiry or other service need. It is one of the important keys to quality service.

The Wandering Customer

Far too often a customer takes his service request to an organization and gets passed from one group or individual to another. With each new person, the customer must explain again what he needs. The customer is very much on his own and not attached to a service provider. No one in the organization has taken ownership for this poor wandering customer. If something positive **does** happen it is probably due to the customer's persistent demand for service rather than to someone stepping up to ownership. There are rumors, unsubstantiated of course, that some customers have been wandering around certain organizations for years looking for someone to take ownership. Sound like an exaggeration? Well, maybe a little. We tend to think this situation occurs only in the large

corporation, but the customer runaround takes place in any size enterprise.

A Customer Problem Means an Opportunity to Take Ownership

First let's consider the customer who has a problem. The attitude of successful service providers is, When my customer has a problem, I have a problem. You accept the problem, and it is yours until a solution is found and the customer is satisfied.

Ownership Confusion

Who owns a customer's problem often causes confusion for customer service providers. The confusion comes when the solution to the customer's problem or other service need falls into a coworker's area of responsibility. Let's use an example to illustrate the point.

A customer calls and describes her service request. The frontline service person immediately recognizes that he can't help the customer and therefore must refer the situation to someone else. Should the frontline person let go of the situation or stay in the loop to make certain the customer is satisfied? It's pretty easy to turn loose of the situation at this point, especially when busy with other customers. The old "not my problem, too busy anyway" syndrome comes into play. But is this the right course to follow?

If the customer or the account is assigned to you, you should continue your involvement. The same is true of a customer with whom you regularly talk. In fact, in most situations your good judgement will tell you to maintain at least enough involvement so that you can monitor the status of the situation.

This is often where more confusion comes into play. How much involvement is required? It varies. You might follow up and report back to the customer at regular intervals. Other times you need only make a simple follow-up telephone call to your colleague who is working on the solution. In some cases, just calling the customer to make certain everything was taken care of will be enough. Regardless of the action taken, the customer must be made to feel the service representative and the organization are looking after her best interest. Staying personally involved provides that comfort for the customer.

Service Must Be Structured for Ownership

A few years ago I conducted customer service training for a well-known organization. Before the training I interviewed employees and managers to increase my understanding of their operation so I could make the training more effective. I quickly learned that both employees and managers agreed their customers were not completely satisfied. However, the exact cause for the poor service was hotly debated within the organization. There was a lot of finger pointing.

As an outsider looking in, I saw that the primary cause of the problem was the way management had designed the customer service system. They had structured service with limited customer ownership and commitment in mind. The service-delivery system worked like this:

• The customer called the service group.

• The Frontline Group answered the call.

• Frontline took the request for service and recorded all the pertinent information. Without making a commitment to the customer, Frontline passed the information to the Tech Support Group.

• Tech Support did one of three things:
  (1) Directly handled the service request
  (2) Passed it to a field technician
  (3) Referred it to the engineering group

This procedure usually took a considerable amount of time. The customer, not knowing what was going on, lost patience and called Frontline again, this time complaining about slow service in addition to the initial problem.

The system was awkward and resulted in many customers being dissatisfied. Clear ownership of the customer's problem or request was missing. The customer was left in the dark because there was little feedback.

In this example, the design of the service system hampered the employee and the organization from satisfying customers. Most of us don't get a chance to design an overall customer-support system. As the customer representative, however, **you** are empowered to design one for your own job. For instance, **you** decide how to manage the support activities that will lead to customer satisfaction. **You** decide to take customer ownership. **You** make the decision to provide quality service. **You** determine when to intercede with other groups or individuals to ensure that your customer is getting the service needed. **You** decide when to provide feedback to the customer. Regardless of the service system design, the customer service responsibility rests in **your** hands.

Frontline Authority Means Responsibility

With this authority comes a second responsibility. You must show the ability to balance all of these customer activities at the same time. It is important to stay focused on your primary mission. Duties include processing orders, discussing services, describing products, troubleshooting problems, managing a large number of calls per day and a multitude of other responsibilities. At the same time, you must take ownership and stay involved in order to satisfy customers. It's not easy.

When the Customer Has Other Service Needs

As a successful service provider, you take ownership when the customer first comes into contact with your organization, regardless of the type of customer

inquiry. Your words and actions immediately assure the customer that her needs will be satisfied.

Most of us have walked into a business or up to a counter and been ignored. We have also called to make an inquiry and been placed on hold for a long time. We wait to be recognized. We wait for someone to step up and take ownership.

We also have been in situations where the representative provided a positive response immediately. His words and actions assured us that ownership had been taken.

A Lack of Ownership Stands Out

It usually doesn't take much for the customer to catch on that ownership hasn't been taken. But the customer most likely won't identify the problem as lack of ownership. Instead, the customer just knows, or has a feeling, that service is deficient. For example, a customer calls to request information. She is told, "Someone will get back to you." There's not much assurance in that statement, and certainly no ownership. Customers want to know **who** is responsible. **Who** will call back. **When** that person will call back. **Who** will come out. **When** will the shipment arrive. When this isn't done, questions and concerns arise about the service. When customers have doubts, they tend to think about taking their business elsewhere.

On the other hand, when ownship is immediately taken, customers feel a sense of security—a feeling they are in capable hands and will be satisfied.

Customers Are Often Reluctant to Call
Frequently, customers dread having to call certain organizations for service. They simply don't want the hassle. One of the chief problems they encounter is

Too often they hear:	When they should hear:
I would like to help but . . .	I'll be glad to help.
I'll have someone call you.	I will check and call you back.
You will have to call _____ .	Let me have _____ call you.
You will have to call the manufacturer.	I'll call and find out.
That's not my job.	Yes, I will personally take care of everything.

the reluctance of someone within the organization to take ownership.

The product explanation. The customer calls and expresses interest in a product but also has some questions and doubts. The representative immediately takes ownership by expertly and patiently answering the questions asked. Her answers are positive, and they reassure and comfort the customer. The customer's doubt about the product is eliminated, and he places an order.

A customer inquiry turns into an order. This is a basic and straight-forward example of satisfying customer needs because someone accepted ownership.

Customers Want Action

Taking ownership is always centered around action. At times that action may be similar to the previous example where customer concerns are satisfied. Other times the action will be to formulate and present an action plan.

Customers want immediate service, and when it can't be delivered, you must present an action plan—a plan that describes to the customer who is taking ownership of his problem, inquiry or other concern and how you will address it. When appropriate, you and the customer might jointly develop this action plan.

Action Plan Ideas:
A complex situation requires an ownership action plan outline consisting of

who, what, when, where, how and even why:

- **Who** is responsible

- **What** is going to happen

- **When** it will happen (the all-important time frame)

- **Where** it will happen

- **How** it will happen

- **What** are the benefits for the customer

- **Why** it will happen

An Action Plan Example
The doctor tells the patient, "Your foot is stuck in your mouth, but don't worry. I'm going to remove it. The operation is set for next Wednesday at 3:00 p.m. at the local hospital. It will be a simple procedure called a foot extraction. It is the only way to remove your foot. Once we have the foot out, you will be able to walk and run again, and the speech problem will go away."

Of course, the kind of plan you provide needs to be adjusted for the type of customer with whom you're working. If the customer likes a lot of detail, then the ownership action plan should have details. If the customer is less "hands on," he may not want to get involved and may require only a brief outline. Others will be gathering information for their boss and may need extra assurance. The bottom line is to keep the customer in mind and present the type of action plan she needs and wants.

Involve the Customer

When it's appropriate, involving the customer in developing an action plan is a good idea. It also works when you are unsure about the exact outcome the customer expects. Ask the customer about his expectations:

> "What would you like to see happen?"

> "How do you feel we can best go about solving this problem?"

> "What would an acceptable plan entail?"

Get Customer Approval
All action plans need customer approval. After you present or develop a plan, obtain agreement. Ownership is complete when you present the action plan and the customer agrees. At this point, you and the customer have formed a partnership. Working as partners is the highest form of customer service.

Conclusion

The introduction to this book mentioned service opportunity and the opportunity individuals and organizations have to excel. By accepting ownership of every customer who enters your organization and providing quality service, you will gain a significant advantage over most of your competitors.

Summary: An Action Plan to Follow

1. Take ownership with the first customer contact.

2. Solve the problem, take the order, and answer the inquiry or present an action plan. In some cases develop the action plan with the customer.

3. Present the action plan's benefits.

4. Obtain the customer's approval of any action plans.

5. Stay involved even though you may not personally resolve the customer's concern.

6. Follow up. Check for customer satisfaction. Don't assume it.

Case Study: The Squeaky Noise

Mary Ellen took in her new car for its first service. She told the service manager she loved the car, but a squeaky noise was driving her crazy. She thought the noise was coming from the dashboard. The service manager said he would take a look at it. When Mary Ellen picked up the car, she noticed the noise problem was noted on her invoice. However, no solution or other comments were written in. The service manager wasn't around, so she asked the cashier whether the noise problem had been fixed. She received an "I don't know; the service manager will be back in a few minutes." Mary Ellen was in a hurry and couldn't wait.

For the next two days Mary Ellen didn't hear the noise and thought the service department had fixed it. Then the noise started again; this time it was even louder. She called the service department and spoke with the service manager, who told her to bring the car in and he would look at it.

Mary Ellen delivered the car to the service department. When she picked up the car, the service manager said he had found a few loose screws in the door panel that were causing the problem. Mary Ellen told the service manager, for the third time, "I'm sure the noise is coming from the dashboard." The service manager said his mechanic found the loose screws in the door panel and that was causing the noise.

To make a long story a little shorter, the noise from the dashboard continued. Each time she had the car serviced Mary Ellen tried to get the service department to find and stop the noise. The service department was always courteous, but never fixed the problem.

After the car's warranty expired Mary Ellen took her car to a small garage a friend had recommended. When she left the car for servicing she mentioned the noise. The owner said she would see if she could find it. When Mary Ellen picked up the car the owner said, "We fixed the dashboard squeak. The back of the glove compartment was slightly loose and rubbing against the dashboard framework.

The mechanic tightened it and we road tested the car and could no longer hear it." The car never squeaked again.

This situation illustrates how one person, the garage owner, accepted ownership of Mary Ellen's problem. She handed off the problem to a mechanic, and then followed through to see that the problem was solved. In contrast, the first service manager never fully accepted ownership. He asked a mechanic to check for a noise, but never personally followed through. He also failed to follow up with Mary Ellen to see if, in fact, the problem was solved. Each time she brought it to his attention he promised to look into it. But Mary Ellen always had to initiate the action.

This type of situation occurs in every business. Not being able to get problems solved is a major reason customers leave and are captured by someone else. Someone must accept ownership of customer problems.

Understanding Your Customer's Business

There are three advantages to understanding the customer's business.

1. You will be of greater service to the customer.

2. The amount of business the customer does with your organization can be increased.

3. As a customer service provider, your value to the customer will be greatly enhanced.

Using Knowledge of the Customer

Suggesting frontline service providers understand their customer's business doesn't mean knowing it inside and out. Instead, the idea is to know enough to be able to expand the need and opportunity for service. Let's look at an example.

Ann West is a customer service representative. She has just taken an order from Sue Brown of the Davis Company.

    Ann: I have everything. Would you like me to go over your order?

    Sue: No, that won't be necessary.

    Ann: I do have a question, if you don't mind.

    Sue: Sure, go ahead.

    Ann: In the past, when you ordered for the branch location you usually ordered for your location as well. I would think by now your inventory might be low.

    Sue: That's a good point. I'll check it.

Not very complicated, was it? Ann knew her customer's usual ordering pattern and consequently demonstrated knowledge of the customer's business.

Here's another example. Ann is talking to customer Tom Craig about an upcoming seminar Ann's organization is conducting.

Ann: Yes, everything is set for the seventh.

Tom: Good. I just wanted to double-check.

Ann: I do have an idea that I think will improve the training.

Tom: What do you have in mind?

Ann: I was thinking maybe we should mix the groups. In reading about your industry I learned there are often communication problems between the technical side of your business and the rest of the organization.

Tom: That's an interesting idea. Frankly, the two groups do have their problems.

Ann knew her customer's business pretty well, and because of that knowledge was able to offer a valuable suggestion. That's quality service.

Three Basic Facts

To have a more thorough understanding of your customer's business there are three basic facts you should know about your customers.

1. Their industry

2. Their business function

3. The application of your products or services

You need the first two facts in order to understand number three, the application of your products or services. By reading about your customer's industry you get the overall picture of the customer's environment. When organizations fall within the same industry group, they normally share many of the same concerns and opportunities, face the same issues and have similar needs.

Industry

Particular industries include retail, wholesale, computers, telecommunications, chemical, financial services, health care and, of course, hundreds of others.

As a service provider you may concentrate on one primary industry or on a broad spectrum. If your customers are from one industry it is easier to understand their overall needs and to become a near-expert regarding their specific industry.

Where do I get this information? Check your library reference desk for useful information. Trade associations and other industry groups usually have literature available for the asking. If you are comfortable doing so, ask your customers for information about their industry and business. Normally, customers will respond in a positive manner and be impressed with your interest.

The Business Function

It's easy to work with customers over a long period of time without ever really knowing much about their business. They call to place an order, make an inquiry or state another service need, and each time you respond with service. The conversation ends and you go on to the next customer. The relationship never moves beyond the normal sequence—customer request followed by a response.

Every business has a primary function. It makes, sells, distributes, processes, services, manages or administers something. Each also has secondary functions. Knowing all of the basic business functions of your customer is a good beginning. With this information you have the "what" of your customer's business.

The "how" of the customer's business is important. The next step is to understand the "how" of the business. This involves the process the customer employs to complete the functions of the business. This is where you normally find the application for your products and services. This is also where you can help the customer because your services or products assist the customer in completing the tasks necessary to perform his business function.

The Application

Think about how your products or services affect the customer's business. Perhaps they reduce costs, improve productivity or just help employees do their jobs. Your services or products have a role in the business. By completely understanding this role you may find expanded opportunities to be of service to the customer.

The benefits. Knowing the customer's business will have a positive impact on your relationship. In the best situation, you will find new applications for services or products. At the least, you will enhance your relationship with the customer because you can intelligently inquire about and discuss her business.

How to Get Started

Below is a customer chart that asks for information about five of your customers. If you know the correct answers, fill in the blanks. If you don't have all the answers, it's time to do some research. First, look at the example. Then create your own chart.

Conclusion

Acquiring an understanding of your customer's industry and business function will lead to new opportunities for your services or products. It also will enhance your customer relationship. Most customer service providers know only the basics about their customer's business. Therefore, this is one more opportunity

EXAMPLE				
Customer	**Industry**	**Business Function**	**Key Issues or Concerns**	**Service or Product Application**
Jones Mfg.	Manufacturing	Produces Widgets	Product Production Costs	We help control costs and provide durable material
Davis Supply	Wholesale	Supplier of Sports Equipment, etc.	Inventory management and sales	Software to control inventory and for account management
YOUR CHART				
Customer	**Industry**	**Business Function**	**Key Issues or Concerns**	**Service or Product Application**

for you to separate yourself from the herd by acquiring an understanding of the customer's business.

Case Study: Michelle Opens a New Account

Michelle had worked for the bookstore for nearly a year. She loved her job. In order to secure more business, the store had begun sending mailers regarding which topics local businesses would like the store to carry. Michelle handled an inquiry from Ann Burns, a customer service manager representing Andrew Financial. Ann was interested in books about customer service. When Michelle asked a few questions, she learned that Ann had been assigned to train a group of new employees. Michelle said she would check with a few publishers and put together a list of titles and call Ann back. Michelle found several books about customer service. She familiarized herself with the books and then decided to do a little more research before calling Ann.

A Little Research Goes a Long Way

In the library, at the business reference desk, Michelle learned that Andrew Financial was a large organization specializing in commercial property and construction loans. A volume titled *Standard and Poor's* said that Andrew Financial was expanding into home mortgage loans, which meant it would employ more customer service people and its expenses therefore were expected to increase dramatically. Initially, Michelle thought she had not learned much and would not be able to use the new information.

She kept the information in mind as she reviewed the books selected for Ann Burns. She thought about those new employees at Andrew Financial and what their jobs would entail. For one thing, Michelle concluded that the service they provide will probably be over the telephone. Next, she thought they would be quoting rates and other cost figures to customers. "Maybe," Michelle thought to herself, "a book covering business math or finance might be appropriate." She found an excellent book called *Basic Business Math*. For the telephone service situation she uncovered another excellent book, *Telephone Courtesy and Customer Service*. Michelle reviewed both books again and decided they might be just what Ann Burns was looking for. She then was ready to call Ann Burns.

Michelle: Ann, I found eight different titles I think you might be interested in.

Ann: Good. I'm looking forward to seeing them.

Michelle: I'll send a pretty complete description of each book.

Ann: Okay. That's exactly what I wanted.

Michelle: I was reading about your company and learned you are getting into the home mortgage business. Is that true?

Ann: Yes, in a big way. I have nearly 30 people to train. That's why I am looking for customer service books.

Michelle: Your trainees will be providing service over the telephone. Is that correct?

Ann: Yes, strictly the telephone.

Michelle: How about their math skills? Will that be something you address during the training?

Ann: Yes, it definitely will be. They will constantly quote rates and payment amounts. They need to be accurate.

Michelle: Included in the list I'm sending are two books I think you will be quite interested in.

Ann: Good. What are they?

Michelle: The first is titled *Telephone Courtesy and Customer Service.* This book gives lots of examples of how to provide quality service over the telephone.

Ann: That sounds perfect. What's the other one?

Michelle: It's called *Basic Business Math,* and it covers the basics of that subject in a step-by-step manner.

Ann: I neglected to mention it to you, but I have been looking for such a book.

Of course, we have a happy ending to our little story. Ann Burns purchased 60 books from the bookstore. Michelle had taken the time to learn a little about the customer's business and then was able to apply it. You can do the same thing.

Don't Share Internal Problems or Information

Very early in the developing years of IBM, employees were instructed not to discuss company business in public. Other organizations followed that example. If you think this issue is not a problem, just tune in and listen the next time you ride an elevator, eat lunch in a crowded place or stand on a busy downtown street corner. Business people often talk as if no one could possibly overhear them or be interested in what they say. They are capable of casually discussing private information about their organization without much thought to who might be listening.

There is a movie starring Peter Strauss called *Kane and Abel* where he plays a waiter in a posh restaurant. He makes money by eavesdropping on his customers. He picks up stock and other financial tips, company gossip and assorted information not meant for his ears.

Most of us don't have to worry about eavesdropping waiters, but the story suggests we keep confidential and other important information about our organization away from outsiders. This is especially true in regards to customer information.

The Customer's Perception

Customers have an image of you and your organization. Hopefully, it's a positive one. This perception was probably created over a long period of time through multiple telephone or face-to-face contacts. To maintain and improve this image, everyone needs to be careful what is said to a customer.

It Doesn't Take Much to Change the Customer's Perception

Most customer relationships are somewhat fragile. They can change rapidly. The customer's perception of your organization can improve or begin to decline depending on what she hears or sees. For example, there are those sudden change-of-policy announcements or price changes that catch customers by surprise. More commonly, your phone rings and an unthinking coworker says, "I am sorry but he's not available. He's in the middle of a big customer problem." The customer begins to wonder about your service.

31

Nearly Everything Influences the Customer's Perception

Everything the customer hears has an impact. A representative complains to a customer about the time she spends in meetings. Suddenly the customer thinks less of the organization. When the customer hears negative comments from employees about their workplace she begins to develop a poor image of the organization.

"Making the Point" and Other Well-Meaning Statements

- **Statement:** To make a point, the representative shares some important information about customer B with customer A.
  Interpretation: Customer A concludes he can't trust the representative.

- **Statement:** Every time the customer calls he hears how busy everyone is.
  Interpretation: The customer doesn't care if you're busy.

- **Statement:** The customer complains about a problem and is told who was responsible.
  Interpretation: The customer doesn't need to hear your internal problems.

- **Statement:** An employee criticizes a coworker in the customer's presence.
  Interpretation: The customer loses respect for the critical employee.

- **Statement:** One employee shares personal information about a coworker when speaking with a customer.
  Interpretation: The customer is embarrassed by this display of inappropriate behavior.

The examples go on, and I'm sure you could add a few of your own. Listen at your office and hear what is being said to customers. Most of us could stand some improvement in this area. Far too

often a slip of the tongue or simply not thinking before speaking creates the wrong impression.

There are five guidelines to follow that will help improve this situation.

GUIDELINES

1. Avoid discussing your organization's business in public.

2. Never share confidential customer information.

3. Personal information about coworkers is just that, personal. Keep it that way.

4. When you're having problems, keep that information within the organization. Don't share it with customers.

5. Support your coworkers, especially with customers.

Conclusion

Measure, monitor and think about everything you say to a customer. Periodically review your conversations to make certain you are meeting the suggested guidelines. Keep in mind that customers have a perception of you and your organization. Continue to enhance that perception by being careful when talking with customers.

Case Study: The Unintentional Comment

Jack had been employed by his firm for several years and liked his frontline customer service job very much. Jack talked to numerous customers every day, and he was always careful of what he said. For example, he was never critical of other employees, departments or his organization. Although there were frequent internal problems because of a major reorganization Jack never shared the "bad news" with his customers.

Jack belonged to a bicycle club. One Saturday the club held a barbecue where a few members got into a discussion regarding good places to work. Jack had experienced a particularly tough week, and he shared some of the problems he found in working for his company. He talked about the reorganization and the problems it had caused and a variety of other concerns including a slowdown in orders. Later a woman approached Jack and said she enjoyed talking with him. In the ensuing conversation he learned the woman's company was considering contracting with Jack's firm. The woman told Jack she found his comments very interesting. "It's always interesting to see things from the inside point of view," she said.

The Point

The point of this situation is basic; you never know who is listening. Keep internal information away from the customers and away from the public.

Self-Improvement

A strong job performance improves customer service. The higher your skill level and the more knowledgeable you are, the more value you add to the customer relationship. Customers prefer to work with highly skilled people. The reason? The transaction or interface usually goes faster, there are fewer errors and the customer can depend on the employee's knowledge and skill. The more complex the situation the more the customer will want to work with this type of representative.

The Outstanding Employee

Look around your organization at the people with whom you work. The strong performers stand out. They have separated themselves from the pack. How are a few employees able to distinguish themselves so well? What do they have that others don't?

Many factors distinguish outstanding employees from the rest, but three stand out. To one degree or another, all employees have and employ the three factors.

THREE FACTORS

1. The education, experience and skills they bring to the job.

2. How readily they apply the organization's formal training, on-the-job training and/or on-the-job observations.

3. Their desire for success and self-improvement.

On day one of a new job, an employee brings a set of skills, an education and usually some experience. The experience may not be in the same type of job but it probably relates in some manner. Your coworkers do the same. Since we have differing amounts of education, experience and skills, we are not exactly equal on this first day. In other words, we are not starting at the same spot.

Training
Your organization provides training either in the classroom, on the job or both. This is where an employee without experience or strong skills can catch up and begin

to pull even or ahead of the competition. Turning in a strong performance in the training classroom or during the on-the-job phase usually attracts attention and provides recognition for the employee because it demonstrates how quickly the individual can absorb new information.

Desire and Self-Improvement

Finally, we get to the great equalizer—desire and self-improvement. The desire to perform and succeed is a power that can overcome many obstacles. A strong desire combined with a self-improvement program is nearly unbeatable. That's a pretty powerful claim, but if you look closely you will find people in your organization who are successful because of their desire to succeed and their self-improvement activities.

Your Self-Improvement Plan

Most employees improve as they gain customer experience, but it's often at a slow or average pace. The learning process and the opportunity to be more successful can be expedited with a well-organized self-improvement program (SIP)—a program designed and implemented by the frontline service provider.

Frequently, this type of program is undertaken at the urging of a supervisor or manager. The supervisor observes an employee's job performance and defines areas that need improvement. A program is drawn, time frames are established and the supervisor monitors and evaluates the employee's progress. At best, the supervisor and the employee interact for the benefit of the employee. At worst, the supervisor uses the improvement program as a punitive measure if the employee fails to meet expectations.

Designed by You for You

The SIP suggested here is different; it's created by you. You monitor and evaluate your own progress. Once you lay out

your SIP you may want to get your supervisor involved for added input and insight.

Benefits for You

Before we discuss how to start your SIP, let's briefly consider what's in it for you.

By focusing on specific areas where improvement is needed you can rapidly advance your performance. There are four personal benefits to a SIP.

1. Others will notice your performance improvement. This means added attention and recognition for you.

2. New or enhanced skills make your job and customer conversations a little easier to manage.

3. Most customer service providers find that the higher their skill level, the more they enjoy customer contacts.

4. The amount of your job satisfaction will increase.

Sounds like four good reasons to get involved in a SIP. Completion of a SIP also means increased satisfaction for your customers. The stronger your knowledge and the higher your skill level, the more likely your customers will be satisfied.

Now the Hard Part

Sometimes it is human nature to sort of hide from the truth. For example, suppose your product knowledge is weak but only you and perhaps a few customers know this. You have a choice: Continue to pretend everything is fine and keep coasting along, or try to improve the situation and include product knowledge in your SIP.

Getting Started

There are four basic steps to creating a SIP.

1. Make a list of the 10 most important skills related to your job.

   EXAMPLES OF SKILLS:
   Verbal Communication
   Listening
   Product Knowledge
   Service Policy Knowledge
   Ability to Manage Stress
   Cultural Awareness
   Understanding Customer's Business
   Providing Added-value Service
   Organizational Ability
   Ability to Meet Time Frames

   These ten are for example only. Select ten skills important to your job and its responsibilities.

   1. _____
   2. _____
   3. _____
   4. _____
   5. _____
   6. _____
   7. _____
   8. _____
   9. _____
   10. _____

2. Rank yourself, using a scale of 1 to 10, on each of the 10 skills.

(1 is low, 5 is average and 10 is high.) Write your rating next to the skill.

3. Select the five lowest-rated skills. These five skills will make up your first SIP.

4. Write the five skills on paper. Next to each skill write an activity designed to help you improve the particular skill. Next to the activity write a date for completion of the improvement activity.

In designing your program try to be as realistic and objective as possible. To verify, ask a coworker, friend or supervisor for their rating of your skills. Establish an activity plan you can complete, and set time frames that you can meet. If you have problems coming up with an activity plan, ask for help. Select a coworker who is good in the particular skill area, and ask for activity ideas. Once you have a written plan, start at once. Stay with it.

The Next Step
When you have completed the first SIP, create a new one by using the next five

---

EXAMPLE SIP

SKILL	SELF RATING	IMPROVEMENT ACTIVITY	COMPLETION DATE
Product Knowledge	4	Read all tech references Discuss with engineers Inquire about training Read customer's product brochures Prepare a note file for ready reference	5 weeks (6/7)
Listening	4	Visit library, find two books on listening Read books and make notes Apply principles and ideas suggested by books	3 weeks (5/20)

skills needing improvement. Complete the same planning steps as before to establish your new SIP. If on the first attempt you made only modest progress on a particular skill, include the skill in the second SIP. Use the same improvement activities or create new ones. The idea is to continue to try to improve and, when needed, try some more.

Summary

Personal desire to succeed is often the basis for success, especially when an individual is willing to change and strive for improvement. The self-improvement plan recommended in this chapter will serve most frontline employees well. Objectively examine your customer skills and determine where improvement is needed. Establish an ongoing self-improvement program to make yourself an even stronger customer service provider.

One final point: keep the SIP as simple and straight-forward as possible. A formal document requiring hours to prepare is not the intent. Write it out on a piece of notebook paper and get started.

Case Study: Mitch Learns Where He Stands

At American Distribution, performance evaluations are formally conducted at the end of every year. Mitch has been with the organization for five years, and each year he was rated a satisfactory employee. As a "satisfactory employee," Mitch receives a year-end salary increase and participates in the company's bonus program. Mitch is satisfied with his position working on the order desk and with the organization. American Distribution is growing at a rapid rate, and new employment positions are opening up.

The company has a policy of promotion from within, but Mitch is still surprised when two of his coworkers are promoted—one to sales and the other to warehouse supervisor.

With these two employees leaving, all the people Mitch started with on the order desk have been promoted or moved on to other jobs. Mitch is now the most experienced employee and the oldest on the order desk, and he isn't sure he likes the feeling. Maybe, he thinks, he should look for other opportunities within the organization.

Talking with his supervisor, Mitch mentions how he feels. The supervisor says, "Why don't you do something about it?" Mitch asks his supervisor what she means. The supervisor explains that several opportunities are coming up, including a new sales position. Mitch has often thought he would someday like an outside sales position. "When a sales position comes up, would you consider submitting my name as a candidate?" he asks. His supervisor replies, "I don't think it would do much good. I doubt they would seriously consider you." Mitch is surprised and asks his supervisor to explain. The supervisor tells Mitch his performance is satisfactory, but the sales group demands more than that.

After a short discussion, the supervisor spells it out for Mitch. She tells Mitch his performance on the order desk would have to be more than just satisfactory. The supervisor says, "For example, your product knowledge would have to improve to be considered for sales. In addition, you will have to demonstrate more interest in sales by upgrading some of your orders and also doing some cross-selling. Your order accuracy also needs improvement." The supervisor went on and spelled out a few other details about Mitch's job performance that required improvement. As the conversation ended the supervisor made it clear to Mitch that his order-desk performance was satisfactory. But to be considered for sales, he would have to undertake a self-improvement program to upgrade his knowledge and skills.

Although Mitch is somewhat negative about the supervisor's remarks, he is fortunate because the supervisor was very direct with him. She pointed out exactly what Mitch must do to be considered for a sales job. If Mitch decides to make his performance stronger, he now knows what to address in his self-improvement plan.

Build Customer Relationships

Even though customer relationships may already be strong, most customer service providers find there is usually room for improvement. This chapter will present three ideas designed to aid in efforts to improve customer relationships.

A strong customer relationship: A relationship in which the customer is completely satisfied, feels appreciated, has learned he can trust and depend on the representative and the services and products offered are reliable.

How many of your customers would state they are completely satisfied? One hopes there are many. The three ideas we are going to discuss will help move more of your customers into the "completely satisfied" column.

THREE IDEAS

1. Show the customer appreciation.

2. Make it easy for the customer.

3. Build trust.

Idea #1: Show the Customer Appreciation

Showing customer appreciation is a simple but effective idea. Taking customers for granted is easy. There is the story of the organization that decided to assign fewer service people to its large accounts. Sales from these large accounts were steady and growing a few percentage points each year. The organization thought the accounts would continue to do the normal amount of business even though fewer service people were assigned. This organization placed more emphasis and assigned additional service personnel to growing the smaller accounts. Several of the large accounts saw this as a sign they were not appreciated, and they began taking their business to the competition.

Provide Assurance
Customers need assurance they are appreciated. No one likes to continue to do business with an organization and feel his or her business is taken for granted.

How about your customers—do they know you appreciate their business? When was the last time you told them?

How to Let the Customer Know

Providing quality service is the first method of showing customer appreciation. Taking care of the customer's order, inquiry, question or problem in an efficient manner sends a strong signal. However, the customer still needs to hear such statements as

> "Thanks for your business. We appreciate it."
>
> "We welcome your business."
>
> "Thanks for selecting us to do business with."
>
> "We appreciate your confidence."

The exact words used are not so important, as long as the **"appreciation"** message gets through. In some situations you can even write the customer a brief letter or note to express your thanks.

Idea #2: Make It Easy for the Customer

The customer's view of service nearly always differs from the service providers'. When frontline service people learn to view their service from the customer's perspective, they usually realize improvement is needed. Learning to perceive service from the customer's viewpoint, therefore, represents a large step toward quality service.

If you were the customer, what would you like changed? One common complaint among customers is, "I wish _____ were easier to do business with." Whereas internally the view is the direct opposite: "We are easy to do business with." In this typical situation the two points of view need to be resolved by accepting the customer's perspective. If the customer feels you are not easy to do business with, then you need to find ways to make things easier for the customer. It's that simple.

Well, Almost That Simple

As you move closer to the customer's service perspective, you may encounter barriers that prevent you from giving the customer everything he or she wants. A compromise can usually be reached whereby the customer is satisfied on most issues. A common example is the inability, because of costs, of the service provider to staff its operation so that every customer receives an immediate answer to his or her inquiry. Service providers just may not be able to return all telephone calls the same day. Nearly all organizations are required to draw limits to their services. Customers generally understand this.

Find the Roadblocks That Prevent Easier Customer Service

To make service easier for the customer, you must identify the roadblocks hindering service and/or effective customer communication. Ideally, the customer will help identify these roadblocks. You can begin this process by asking a few customers, "Do you find us easy to do business with?" "In what ways are we hard to work with?" and "What roadblocks do you see that hinder service?" Involving the customer will help build a stronger relationship. In a sense, involving the customer places the two of you in a sort of partnership—a partnership formed to help solve problems. Often these problems—the roadblocks—are completely within the service provider's control.

After you have talked with a few customers and given the matter some thought, make a list of the roadblocks mentioned. Set about removing them or at least reducing their impact.

Examples of roadblocks. In addition to asking for the customer's suggestions, the place to start may be your self-improvement program. Are any of your self-improvement areas also roadblocks to effective customer communication? If so, concentrate on those skills along with those identified by customers. Use an approach similar to the one on page 34. Identify the roadblocks that hinder customer communication and service. Next, determine a process that will help you remove them. Let's consider two common examples of roadblocks.

Remembering Conversations

Most customer service employees talk with many customers per day. It is often difficult to recall the details of a customer conversation from several days earlier. However, customers expect the service person to remember the previous conversation. Even a few days later, the customer begins the conversation as a near continuation of the previous one, and when the service provider cannot remember the details of the prior discussion, the customer is forced to repeat what was said. Customers grow tired of restating their request or inquiry. If you face this problem, the solution might be note-taking. Simply refer to the notes when the customer calls back, and eliminate a roadblock.

A CSR kept a small notebook with her at all times. She made quick notes on every one of her customer conversations. The next time she met or talked with the customer she knew exactly what was said during the previous conversation. Customers were impressed with her memory and attention to detail.

Another Example: Telephone Tag

The customer gathers the details needed to make his inquiry or to place an order. He calls and gets a message—you are unavailable. You call back and get a message that he is away from his desk. He calls back and . . . Sometimes it goes on and on until finally the next day or the day after you are both available at the same time and you finally talk. This scenario goes on every day in most organizations. It is poor customer service, and there is something you can do about it.

It's Your Responsibility

The customer call is your responsibility. Anyone can play telephone tag because it requires no skill and leads everyone in circles. Taking responsibility means you will call the customer back as soon as possible. When one call ends, check for customer messages that came in while you were on the phone. Make any callbacks immediately because the customer is probably at her desk, since she just called a few minutes earlier. If she is not there, ask what time would be best to call back. Leave word that you will call at the specific time. Follow up and meet that commitment. When following up a customer call, keep in mind it is your responsibility to contact the customer, not the customer's responsibility to contact you. Customer telephone callbacks are often a roadblock, but like other aspects of the frontline job, they can be managed. Accept the responsibility and make it easier for the customer.

Idea #3: Build Trust

Just a brief word about trust. Customer surveys tell us that strong relationships are based on trust. The customer wants and needs to trust you. He wants to trust the accuracy of the information you provide. She needs to be able to rely on your words and promised actions. Often the customer cannot do his work without accurate input from you. If the customer receives poor or inaccurate information, then she loses trust in you—and even your organization.

Another Trust Situation, Worth Mentioning

Often the customer is gathering information for someone else in his organization.

How often do you hear the following? "My boss wants to know such and such." "My supervisor asked me to call." "We are working on this project and need some figures from you." If the customer has incorrect information, she often winds up embarrassed in front of the boss or her coworkers. This embarrassment means the customer will no longer trust the service provider who supplied the incorrect information.

How to Improve Customer Trust

For customer service providers there are **two** actions that provide much of the basis for customer trust.

1. **Meet commitments.** Whatever you promise the customer, make certain it can be delivered. Whether it be a telephone callback or a lengthy report, meet the time frame promised. An old adage applies here: **PROMISE ONLY WHAT YOU CAN DELIVER, AND DELIVER WHAT YOU PROMISE.**

2. **Be accurate.** If you quote prices or costs or other pertinent information, make certain you are correct. The customer often shares information with others, and therefore it is especially important for the frontline person to be accurate. The customer probably needs your accuracy to make his work accurate.

Summary

Adding strength to your customer relationships is an ongoing process. This chapter suggested three ideas that add to the relationship. Show customer appreciation, make it easy for the customer to do business with you, and build trust. Define roadblocks that interfere with quality service and reduce or remove them. With fewer roadblocks the customer will find you easier to do business with. Customer trust is the cornerstone of the relationship. Trust can be built by meeting all customer commitments.

Case Study: Showing Appreciation Pays

As a CSR, Sally handled all government accounts. The government paperwork and purchasing procedures were complicated for most CSRs, but Sally understood them perfectly. One of her important customers was a woman named Cynthia at the Department of Defense with whom Sally had worked for a long time. Cynthia was formal in her conversation and usually talked only about business. Sally was far from the serious type, but when she spoke with Cynthia she tried to match her customer's behavior and conversational tone.

One day, following a typical order from Cynthia, Sally decided to write a note. In the note she thanked Cynthia for all the business and commented on how much she enjoyed talking and working with her. The note was simply an expression of appreciation. A couple of weeks went by, and Sally never gave the note another thought. Then she received a letter from Cynthia. The letter said nothing about the note. Instead, it listed five different government purchasing agents whom Cynthia knew. Her letter said she had recommended Sally and her organization to the purchasing agents and suggested that Sally call them.

Sally followed up. Four of the five agents wanted catalogs. Within a few weeks Sally started receiving purchase orders from the four agents. Sally increased the number of government orders by nearly 10 percent in the first year.

All this started with a note to one customer expressing appreciation for her business.

Know Your Competition

When was the last time you saw the competition? Have you ever seen them? Do you know anyone who works for your largest competitors? Sure, you probably see their advertisements, their buildings, brochures and maybe even trucks or cars with their name on the side. However, you probably know very little of a personal nature about them. For example, could you answer these questions?

• What is it like to work for them?

• What do they think of your organization?

• Do they discuss your organization in their meetings?

Your Customer, Their Customer

The one thing you know for certain is that your competition has a few of your organization's customers and you have a few of theirs. There are only so many customers out there, and many of them are shared from time to time. A customer locks into your business, likes the service, products and prices. Suddenly one day, or after a period of problems, she becomes dissatisfied and moves to the competition. Maybe the customer did not feel appreciated or became dissatisfied for another reason, or perhaps the competitor presented his case extremely well. No matter the cause, the customer is gone, and you or someone in your organization has to go get one of their customers in order to maintain the balance. When you lose customers and fail to pick up new ones, you lose market share to the competition. Clearly, this hurts you and helps the competitors.

Once a Customer Leaves, It's Hard to Get Him Back

It takes a long time, if ever, to get customers back. Hanan and Karp in their book *Customer Satisfaction* refer to losing a major customer. "It may take three to five years to become competitive again with a dissatisfied customer who has sought satisfaction elsewhere. Meanwhile, someone else's key customer will have to be captured." Sounds like a game, doesn't it? You capture a customer like a chess piece and protect the rest of your customers from being captured. It is a game in a way. A deadly serious game.

The Defense
The best defense against losing any customer is to provide quality service. Incorporated into that quality is knowledge of your competitors. If you know a lot about your competitors, the subject of competition probably comes up several times a day during customer conversations. If you know little about your competitors, the subject is probably not discussed at all. Think about the previous two statements. Which statement best describes your service? Being well informed about the competition is essential because your customers need to hear about your competitors from you.

A Situation
Imagine a customer, your customer. She decided to do business with your organization. Over a long period she is satisfied with your service and has found she can depend on you. Your competitors would like to have this customer for their own, so they call her, send her letters and advertisements, invite her to seminars and other special events. They

want her business. One day she gets curious and asks you about their services. "How do they compare?" she asks. "What advantages do you have over them?" she wants to know. How well can you answer the questions?

A Moment of Panic
For too many service people it is truly a moment of panic because they don't know enough about the competition to accurately answer the questions. A few moments into the conversation the customer senses this lack of knowledge and drops the questioning. The customer, if curious enough, will find out for herself by calling your competitor. The customer's business is at risk and the competition is poised to capture.

A Different Moment
Suppose, instead of the scenario we just examined, the representative was knowledgeable about the competition. When the customer asked questions about the competition the representative discussed services by comparing and contrasting the two organizations, all the time emphasizing the benefits of his service. The customer now has the answers she wants and unless there was other motivation, probably would not contact the competition.

A Benefit to Knowing the Competition

Knowing about your competitors offers an interesting benefit. If a customer is satisfied with the organization's service but asks questions about the competition, he will normally accept the answers offered and not contact the competition. If, on the other hand, a customer is not satisfied you can plan on her contacting the competition, almost regardless of how you answer her questions. Now for the third part. When a representative cannot answer a customer's questions about the competition, you can count on the customer contacting the competitor. From this we can conclude that a service provider must be knowledgeable about the competition in order to satisfy customer needs and keep the customer captured.

Reinforce the Customer's Decision

At some point, your customer decided to do business with your organization. Every time the customer contacts you or places an order, she reaffirms that decision. When inquiries about the competition arise, you need to be able to show that your service and your organization are superior to the competition. By doing this successfully, you accomplish two very important objectives. First, you satisfy the customer because you have the answers. Second, by presenting your organization in a favorable light, you reinforce the decision the customer made to do business with you in the first place. Think how you feel when a business decision you made is complimented and therefore reinforced by a peer or superior. It's the same thing with the customer.

Getting Ready

A service provider needs to do three things in order to be prepared for most inquiries about competitors.

1. Know how to compare and contrast services, products and other important factors of your organization to the competitors.

2. Be able to emphasize the benefits of doing business with your organization.

3. Maintain a competition file.
   - Have everyone in the office contribute
   - Keep it current
   - Share competitive information with others

Where to Start

Start by finding out what you know about the competition. Below is a generic example of a competition chart. You will want to alter it for your own purposes. The idea is to record pertinent facts about those key players who are trying to capture your customers. Once you have tried to complete the chart, you will know how much you know about your major competitors.

Be sure to modify the chart for your own purposes. Include all pertinent information—especially other factors the customers might be interested in or could ask about. Most people find that sections of their chart have little or no information. This is the time to conduct some research.

	Products/ Services Offered	Service	Price	Warranty	Features
COMPETITION CHART EXAMPLE					
Your organization	ABC Model	full support	$$$$	2 years	11 features state of the art
Competitor 1	XYZ Model	contract to others	$$$$$	1 year	9 features
Competitor 2	XXX Model	no support	$$$	18 months	old technology

Research Sources

Good sources are available for your research. Start with your own organization. Ask whether a competition file already exists. Check the library reference desk for information about individual competitors. Look at their annual reports to get an overall feel for the organization. Ask former customers of the competition—those whom you captured—about their experience with the competitor. Read the business section of your local newspaper. Write for information in response to ads; call the competition's toll-free number and request literature and other promotional materials. In short, learn as much as possible. The more you know, the better service you will be able to provide.

Summary

Competitive knowledge is essential. To provide complete service for your customer, you must be able to discuss competitors. Know how to compare and contrast their services and products to yours. Be able to show the benefits of your organization that major competitors don't offer. A competition file for your work group is a must. If you already have a file, make certain it is kept updated. If you don't have one, it's important to establish one.

Case Study: Undoing the Competitor

Jennifer works in customer service at the Paulson Furniture Company, which manufactures and sells furniture. She was asked by one of the salespeople, Dave Miller, to complete a request for proposal (RFP) that he had received from a major hotel. When Jennifer asked a few questions about how the RFP should be prepared, Dave said, "Just fill in the spaces. We don't stand a chance of getting our furniture in that hotel. They

think we are too high priced." Jennifer asked, "If that's the case, why are we bothering to complete the RFP?" Dave smiled and said, "My boss wants us to respond to all RFPs."

Jennifer looked at the RFP and concluded it was pretty standard—with one major exception. She noticed the hotel was asking for prices and fabric selections on 30 oversized five-cushion sofas along with 50 oversized three-cushion sofas. Jennifer thought this request was odd. These sofas were very heavy and therefore awkward to move, and most hotels went with lighter furniture. She concluded that some interior designer had a certain look in mind and had sold the idea to the hotel. Still curious, she mentioned the RFP and the sofa request to Amanda, a coworker. Amanda said, "It sounds like one of those RFPs prepared by Frame Furniture." Jennifer was familiar with Frame Furniture but didn't understand Amanda's remark. "What do you mean?" she asked. Amanda explained: "Frame Furniture is very active in the hotel/motel market, and one of their sales tactics is to offer a hotel's management assistance with the RFP. They use a standard RFP format and include their own hotel furniture specifications wherever the customer will allow it. That way, we wind up bidding directly against their products." Jennifer understood and replied, "Of course, they offer lower prices, especially on those large sofas." Amanda agreed and then said, "Sure. Price is a big factor. Why else would they include that elephant furniture?" Jennifer and Amanda both laughed at the joke.

Jennifer was intrigued by the way her competitor worked. She decided to learn more. Since the RFP was due in a few days she would have to hurry. She found a current Frame Furniture catalog in the office and examined it closely. She noticed that some of Frame Furniture's prices were lower, but not so low that Jennifer felt she couldn't compete. Frame did, however, offer an inferior fabric selection. Jennifer's company offered both higher-quality fabric and a much larger selection.

In talking with another coworker Jennifer learned that Frame only offered financing through a finance company, while Jennifer's company provided short-term financing at current interest rates. Jennifer immediately checked with her finance department and learned what kind of terms she might offer the hotel. Jennifer didn't know if the financing information would come into play or not, but it was good to have it just in case.

Jennifer was then ready to call the hotel's headquarters. She asked for a Ms. R. Bradshaw, whose name was on the RFP. Jennifer introduced herself to Ms. Bradshaw and engaged her in conversation about the RFP. At one point Jennifer said, "I was surprised to see the request for the oversized sofas. Usually hotels find these too heavy and awkward because they always have to be moved around." Ms. Bradshaw said she agreed and told Jennifer the interior designer had suggested the sofas and that was the only reason they were in the RFP. Ms. Bradshaw said the hotel wasn't sure it would use the oversized sofas. "We might buy a lighter, less-bulky model," she said. Jennifer mentioned the financing she had to offer and Ms. Bradshaw said the hotel would be interested, and requested additional information. Jennifer

promised to send a letter explaining the terms and conditions her company offered. Jennifer asked if it was okay to call the designer and discuss the sofas. Ms. Bradshaw thought that was a good idea and provided a name and telephone number.

The designer liked the oversized sofas but was pretty certain the hotel had decided against them. Jennifer described the sofas that her company offered and emphasized the large fabric selection. The designer wanted to see a catalog and fabric samples, so Jennifer called Dave Miller, told him what was going on, and then included him in a conference call with the designer so an appointment could be set.

Following the call, Jennifer told Dave about the RFP situation, her conversation with Ms. Bradshaw, and the letter she promised to send. Dave said he would send a letter regarding the finance and then follow up.

It took another six weeks before the hotel made a decision, but it was worth the wait: The hotel decided to place most of its furniture order with Paulson Furniture Company. Dave Miller made a big sale with a lot of help from Jennifer. Or was it the other way around?

In this example Jennifer was far from being an expert regarding her competitor, Frame Furniture. However, she learned enough to set in motion a possible sale.

Mental Scripting

Are you one of those people who always has an answer for any question or situation? If you are, congratulations. If not, there is a way to acquire that skill, the skill of having a prepared response to the customer's inquiry or statement. It's called mental scripting.

In mental scripting, successful salespeople and others visualize in advance what a meeting with the customer will be like. They think about where everyone will sit, how they will act, and what they will say. Good salespeople also anticipate questions or objections that might come up. To be prepared, they rehearse by visualizing the customer offering an objection and then how they will respond in a positive manner. Service providers need to do the same thing. Before we go any further, let's define mental scripting.

Mental Scripting: Preparing, practicing and memorizing a complete response based on a particular statement, question or objection from the customer. Sometimes, scripting key words instead of a complete response works just as well.

With experience, most service providers learn to script certain responses mentally without being aware of it. They hear the same questions over and over from customers. The service provider listens to the question and automatically reacts with a mentally scripted response that satisfies the customer. The response normally emphasizes benefits to the customer and presents the service provider's organization in the best light. The purpose of mental scripting is to deliver the best possible response to the customer. Here's an example.

Let's suppose each day you are asked several times by different customers why your prices are higher than your competitor's. Rather than being put on the defensive, you develop a standard "scripted" reply that answers the question and satisfies the customer.

> **Customer:** Why are your prices higher than others?
>
> **Frontline:** When you consider the services we provide, I think you will find our prices compare very well. Our warranty period is a full two years instead of the usual 18 months. That means added protection and possible savings for you. Would you like to discuss the maintenance plan?

This reply answers the questions and, at the same time, states the benefits of your service. The response is complete and should satisfy the customer.

Scripting Gives You Control

Mentally scripting answers to certain customer responses, questions or statements is worthwhile. By scripting your response, you will be sure to include all the information the customer needs and, at the same time, all the details you want to present. This approach provides more control because you know exactly what you are going to say and even when you're going to say it. Often, as in the example, a short response suffices.

Think of all the repetitive customer statements, questions and objections you hear on an ongoing basis. Your response to each customer is probably a little different. Most service providers offer an excellent response to one customer, a good response to others and occasionally forget to include an important detail with some. Other times, you give a customer more than she wants. Use mental scripting, and all of your responses can be excellent.

How to Start

To begin, make a list of the ten most common questions, statements or objections you hear from customers. Here are ten examples.

1. How do your costs compare?

2. Why does service take so long?

3. Who are your key competitors?

4. The contract is confusing.

5. How does the product work?

6. I'll have to think about it.

7. I think I'll shop around before I decide.

8. What's the difference between the two service plans?

9. What does the warranty cover?

10. Can you explain how your emergency service works?

Of course, these questions and statements are generic, but a few probably apply to your situation. After you have made your list, the next step is to begin mentally scripting an answer to each one.

Creating the Script

The script you create should consist of four ideas. First, answer the customer's question. Next, state your benefits and/or other important facts. Third, ask a question that pertains to the customer's request and is designed to keep the conversation moving in the direction you want. Finally, keep it short, because the customer is probably more interested in facts presented in a concise manner.

Examples

Keep in mind, the customer is thinking about her statement or question and deserves an immediate response before you state benefits and include other important information. Here's an example:

Customer: What is the difference between your two products?

Frontline: [Answer the question first. Then continue:] There are many differences, but basically the 812 will improve your productivity because it is nearly twice as fast. The 812 is an advanced version of the 811 and also includes seven new features.

Would you like me to go over the features and discuss how they apply to your operation?

Let's look at another example of answering the question, stating benefits and then asking an appropriate question to involve the customer.

Customer: Would you explain how your service works?

Frontline: Sure, I'd be glad to. We have a service center that is available to you 24 hours a day, 7 days a week. We are the only organization in the industry offering this service. You just call our 800 number. Does this service sound like something you could use?

Scripting is not intended to remove the spontaneity or enthusiasm from your response. Instead, it is a proven and successful method of having a prepared response ready for delivery when the customer asks a particular question, makes a statement or offers an objection.

Summary

Mental scripting works! It's an easy method of insuring you deliver the right response to the customer. Provide a response that answers the customer's question, offers information in an organized manner and states the benefits of your service.

Case Study: Nancy and the Note Cards

When it came to service and product knowledge Nancy knew more than nearly everyone else. She excelled in training and was always the first one to read about new services. Most customers appreciated her in-depth knowledge, but Nancy was aware she often talked beyond the point and provided too much information.

Nancy read about mental scripting and decided to give it a try. To start, she considered the services she described every day to customers. Using note cards, she listed the key points about each service and then mentally rehearsed short verbal descriptions that included the points.

At first it seemed awkward, and Nancy felt she wasn't giving the customers enough information. But after a week or so she realized her customers were just as satisfied as before. One thing immediately surprised her: She was spending less time on the telephone. She concluded maybe she had been providing, as suspected, too much information.

Nancy also learned that by asking an appropriate question following her mentally scripted response those customers who wanted more information would ask for it, indicating they wanted the conversation to continue.

After just a few weeks, Nancy noticed she had misplaced her note cards. At first she began to search, but then realized everything was mentally scripted and she no longer needed the cards.

Develop Superior Product and Service Knowledge

Whether an organization offers services, products or both, the frontline service provider **must** be an expert regarding these offerings. Customers want and expect this expertise, and when it is provided the customer receives added value and the relationship is enhanced.

When the service provider's knowledge level is high, the customer becomes more dependent on the service person because she learns she can rely on the advice and counsel given. The customer and the service person work in a sort of shirt-sleeve environment; stiffness leaves the conversation as each becomes at ease with the other. The two of you trust and mutually count on this new relationship, which has you working together to resolve customer problems or concerns, such as reducing expenses or improving productivity. At the same time, the amount of business the customer does with your organization usually increases.

The Moment of Truth

Author Karl Albrecht in his excellent book *The Only Thing That Matters* talks about the moment of truth, when the customer first makes contact. This critical moment is a great opportunity to begin the process of capturing or recapturing a customer. Recapturing brings added value and satisfaction to an existing customer. As discussed before, your customer has made a decision to do business with you. The customer deserves to have that decision validated by your delivery of quality service. The new customer is captured with your expanded knowledge and its application to his business.

A Few Stand Out

In every work situation, a few service employees stand out because they know more than anyone else about the services and products offered. These are the people of whom everyone asks questions about products, service, and organizational policy or procedures.

Customers prefer these knowledgeable employees. They like these employees because they seldom hear, "I'll have to check and call you back," or "That's a good question. Can you hold on while I get you an answer?" or "I don't know. Let me get someone to help you."

Many service providers get by with just a basic knowledge of services and products. They have learned that this level of knowledge serves them well in providing service for the average customer. However, their customers recognize the limitation of doing business with a nonexpert. The customer knows that this basic-knowledge-only service provider does not offer added-value service. The customer hears few, if any, suggestions or creative ideas from this person.

Service Is Limited by Knowledge

Lack of knowledge limits the depth of your service. If you don't understand the customer's business very well and have a limited knowledge of your own services and products, your value to the customer is greatly diminished. You may be able to get by, but your success will be limited.

Acquiring a high level of knowledge and offering value-added service to customers is what the service job is all about. When you reach the plateau of combining excellent customer skills with in-depth service and product knowledge, you have placed yourself in the top 10 percent of all service providers. It is a goal worth striving for.

How to Improve

You need to develop and implement a plan, similar to the self-improvement plan discussed in chapter 7, to improve

product and service knowledge. It should have two steps: First, evaluate your knowledge level. Second, develop an action plan for improvement.

The Self-Evaluation
Make a list of all services and products you have responsibility for and usually discuss with customers. Alongside each entry, rate yourself on a 1 to 10 basis. (1 is poor and 10 is excellent.) If you work primarily with products, list those first. If you work for a service organization, start with the most important aspect of service you offer. The following is an example.

Example. Since we are all familiar with banks, let's look at how a bank employee, who works with customers, might approach the self-evaluation.

SELF-EVALUATION	
Services Provided	**Rating of Knowledge Level and Ability to Discuss with Customers**
Checking Accounts	9
Checking Accounts for people older than 55 years	9
Interest-Paying Checking Accounts	7
Minimum Balance	8
No-Service-Charge Checking Accounts	7
Regular Savings Account	10
Certificates of Deposit (CD)	7
Individual Retirement Accounts (IRA)	6
Christmas Club Savings	10
Consumer Loan Rates and Procedures	5
Mortgage Loan Rates and Procedures	6
Functions of the Trust Department	2
How We Compare/Contrast with Other Banks	2

The Action Plan

Following the self-evaluation, you must establish an action plan similar to the self-improvement plan we discussed earlier. In our example, the bank employee looks like a lot of service providers—strong in certain areas and weak in others. To develop an action plan for improvement, it's important to also establish priorities for those areas rated. The highest priorities are the areas customers inquire about the most. For example, our bank employee's self-rating is a 2 in knowledge of the trust department. Although this rating needs improvement, the employee may not be asked about the trust department very often. Therefore, the requirement for strong knowledge in this area is not as important as some others. Inquiries about the different types of checking and savings accounts, on the other hand, are probably in constant demand. So the action plan might begin with a program designed to increase checking and savings account knowledge. Eventually, the low priorities are taken into consideration and their ratings are improved as well.

The Next Step. The next step is to determine activities that will allow you to improve each rating. In some cases it may be reading about services and products, asking questions, participating in formal training or observing coworkers who are more skilled. Whatever activity you decide upon, it's important to get it under way.

Summary

Being an expert about your products and services is essential. The customer wants and expects it. All customers have one thing in common: They want to work with knowledgeable people, and they want their questions answered with accuracy. A service provider with a great deal of job knowledge adds value for the customer.

Case Study: Tracy Finds the Perfect Customer

Tracy's supervisor approached her one day and asked if she would take over a particularly difficult account. It seemed everyone considered Mr. Donovan from Adams Electronics as almost too demanding to do business with. Tracy knew her supervisor was just being polite by asking if she wanted the account; it was really a new assignment.

Tracy looked over the account information. She had heard Mr. Donovan's name impolitely bandied about the office on certain occasions, and she wondered how she was going to manage to get along with him. Tracy called Mr. Donovan and arranged for a meeting with him at his office.

When she met Mr. Donovan, Tracy was surprised to find him very polite and cordial. He explained his duties as the MIS director of Adams Electronics and how he personally ordered most of the equipment the organization needed. Mr. Donovan was quite candid about the problems he had had with Tracy's organization. He cited numerous circumstances where he had been given the wrong information. But he was still doing business with her company because he thought many of the products were superior.

Tracy responded with a few statements to show how well she understood the need for accuracy. She then asked, "How can I help you at the present time?" Donovan replied that the project he was concerned about at the moment was a modem* analysis. Tracy asked about the

---

*modem: a communication device used in the transmission of data, it modulates and demodulates the signal

type and speed of the modems he was considering and their application. Mr. Donovan showed her a spreadsheet he was working on that, when complete, would depict all the modem information he needed on a single page. He asked Tracy if she would do some research and fill in the blanks regarding her company's modems. Tracy replied she knew the information he needed and didn't need to conduct research. On the spot she filled in the blanks as Mr. Donovan watched and asked questions as she proceeded. When she was through, they began discussing the competitors and Tracy filled in many of those spreadsheet blanks as well. Mr. Donovan was impressed with Tracy's excellent product knowledge and her accuracy. He immediately found her to be a valuable resource.

Be Proactive with Customers

Being proactive with customers means taking the initiative. For our purposes, let's define the word initiative.

Initiative: The power or ability to begin or follow through with a plan or task that benefits the customer

---

This definition contains several key words worth discussing. First, the definition begins with the words "power or ability." As a service provider, you have the power to take initiative and to be proactive on behalf of your customer. This power and authority to take action is inherent in your job. You don't need permission to exercise it. You also have the ability to recognize those customer situations calling for proactive behavior.

Next in the definition are the words "plan or task." Your proactive behavior is plan- or task-driven. You initiate an action or task as part of a plan. Whether you finish a task as a stand-alone action or as part of a much larger customer-satisfying plan, both are designed to benefit the customer.

Benefits for You

Being a proactive service provider adds to your overall effort to provide quality service. Customers no longer have to wait for action or decision or wonder who's in charge. Your proactive performance means you recognize and act upon the opportunity for service. When you constantly take a proactive stance, the customer learns to depend on your services and perceives you as capable and someone who can be trusted to take the necessary action. When the customer's perception is this strong, you are in the top 10 percent of all customer service providers—an excellent place to be.

Eight Opportunities

The following customer situations describe opportunities for proactive service. The purpose is to illustrate the opportunity for proactive behavior in everyday customer situations. Included with each opportunity is a plan or task that, when implemented, will result in proactive service. These tasks come with a guarantee: They will increase the amount of satisfaction your customer receives. Keep in mind the situations shown are only a partial list of the many opportunities you have for proactive service.

1. The Customer Callback

You know all those telephone messages you receive for customer callbacks? For example, when you are talking with a customer on the telephone and other customers' calls continue to stack up? Most service providers have a tendency to let the messages pile up and answer them when there is more time. It's important to think of the customer who leaves a message as someone who deserves immediate service. The longer it takes to receive attention the more her dissatisfaction grows. Be proactive by returning customer telephone calls as soon as possible.

2. The Customer with a Problem

Earlier, in talking about taking ownership, we stressed that immediate action is required when the customer has a problem. This "problem" situation is critical and worth added discussion, for it is at this time that the customer is at risk and you are in danger of losing him. Immediate proactive service is required to reduce the risk. You can be proactive regarding customer problems in three distinct ways.

1. Make certain you immediately share the customer's concern and sense of urgency. How? Convincingly inform the customer you understand the importance of the problem and how urgent the solution is.

2. When the problem is not resolved promptly, provide the customer with feedback and status reports. Discuss what is going on and provide assurance the problem will be resolved. Allow the customer to contribute ideas and suggestions.

3. When a problem has a serious negative impact upon the customer's business, develop a plan to prevent a recurrence. Be proactive by offering such a plan. The customer should have a role in the formation of the plan and also the right to approve it. Without customer concurrence any plan is meaningless.

When put into practice, these three proactive ideas will help the customer through the problem situation and provide the needed assurance. One last word on the third item: By suggesting that a plan be developed to prevent a problem from recurring, do not necessarily offer a formal presentation to the customer. Instead, keep it simple and direct. For example, devise appropriate guidelines that will prevent future mistakes, review them with the customer, get her agreement and make certain they are adhered to.

3. Proactively Contact the Customer

Being proactive also means occasionally contacting customers instead of waiting to see if they are going to call. When employees, who carry the responsibility for service, hear this idea, they sometimes glaze over in a look of utter disbelief. They exclaim, "Who has time to initiate calls?" or "I have enough calls to manage. I don't need more work."

The suggestion is made because there are numerous situations when a follow-up is appropriate. Here are two examples:

Two circumstances when proactive is needed.
1. The unscheduled follow-up call.
   e.g., "When we last talked you were considering changing your service agreement. I haven't heard from

anyone in your organization and thought I should call to double-check."

2. Several days following the resolution of a customer problem.
  e.g., "I wanted to make certain there have been no further problems."
  e.g., "How is everything working?"

4. Share New Information
When your organization announces changes in policy, prices, service plans or any other customer offering, your key customers deserve to hear the news. If you think they will be interested or can otherwise use the new information, notify them by telephone, fax or letter of the changes.

Key customers deserve to get the news before the general customer base, and they should hear it from their representative. Use this opportunity to be proactive.

5. Contact Former Customers
When your organization has news that affects customers, you have an opportunity to contact those customers you haven't heard from in a while. Be proactive and call to let them know about the changes and ask if you can be of assistance. Of course, this is also a good time to learn what the customer has planned for the future and whether your organization might fit in. This may also be an appropriate time to discuss why the customer hasn't conducted any business with your organization in a while—perhaps there is an unresolved problem or other misunderstanding that needs to be discussed.

6. Eliminate Customer Anxiety
Think how many times your customers may feel anxious. For example, following a conversation the customer may feel a certain amount of urgency. He may be waiting for his bill to be corrected, for information, for packages or shipments, for important dates or schedules from

your organization. During these times, the customer may experience some anxiety, because work may be held up until he receives information from your organization.

During such times, there is usually a point where you have information the customer doesn't have. You know when the shipment was sent, for example. Often, these events represent an opportunity for proactive service. Call the customer and tell him what has taken place. Reducing customer anxiety is a solid way to provide quality proactive service and to build trust.

7. Follow Up with the General-Inquiry Customer
Think of all the calls you receive each day. Many of these people are first-time callers, often just making a basic inquiry. You provide a response, the conversation ends and that is the last you hear from this customer or potential customer. Depending on your business, you may receive a large number of such calls per day. If so, keep track of any inquiry-type calls that are different from the average inquiries where the customer expressed strong interest in your services or products, where the conversation was longer than most or where a particular rapport seemed to be established.

When time permits and after an appropriate interval, follow up with these customers. When calling, you can normally just introduce yourself and ask if there are any additional questions or if the customer has made a decision. By following this proactive suggestion, you will be surprised by the number of new customers captured over a period of time.

8. Follow Up Customer Mail with a Telephone Call
Another good opportunity for proactive service is the literature and other mail many customer service providers send to

59

customers. A customer calls and requests information. You mail a brochure or other information. Often you never hear from the customer again.

Make it a personal rule to follow up on any mail you send to customers. See if the customer has any questions or wishes to discuss any particular points. This follow-up is extra service and definitely adds value to the relationship.

Wrap-Up

The opportunities for proactive service are numerous. Those listed here are only a few examples of the opportunities frontline service has to be proactive. The biggest problem for most service providers is **time.** Where do I get the time to do all this follow-up? It's not easy, but try to develop a plan to make a few such calls per day. You will be pleasantly surprised by the results.

Summary

Providing proactive service is something that average service providers don't do. Most wait for the customer to take action. Being proactive separates you from the rest. Look for opportunities to contact the customer and provide value-added service.

Case Study: Customers Waiting to Be Called

Beach Software, Inc. was a growing organization. Its sales-lead generation focused on trade-show participation and magazine advertising. Each one of these sources produced numerous leads—customers filled out a response card requesting additional product information. As the response cards arrived, a product brochure was immediately mailed to the customer. The weakness of the lead-generation program was the lack of

follow-up with the customers after the brochures were sent.

The salespeople believed most response cards were turned in by people just looking for file information. So they sorted through the response cards and selected the so-called "hot leads" and called them. Things were hectic at Beach Software, and no one had either the time or interest to call the hundreds of leads the salespeople didn't think were worthwhile. Besides, the salespeople said, the response-card customers would call if interested.

Finally, Mavis, the customer service manager, decided something had to be done. She selected two of her people and asked them to start calling **all** the response-card customers. Together they worked out a short telephone script: the CSR would call, provide an introduction, explain this was a follow-up call to the customer's request for a brochure, thank the customer for his or her interest and ask if there were any questions.

The two CSRs began their calling. Mavis asked them to log the results of each call in one of four categories.

1. **Order Taken**

2. **Referred to Sales for Follow-Up**

3. **Customer Not Interested**

4. **Could Not Reach Customer/Left Message**

At the end of five days of calling, Mavis and her two CSRs met to look at the results. The sales manager joined them. Out of 320 calls made, the results were as follows:

1. **Orders Taken: 9 ($22,500 in gross sales)**

2. Referred to Sales for Follow-Up: 25

3. Customer Not Interested: 158

4. Could Not Reach Customer/Left Message: 128

After reviewing the results, the sales manager thanked Mavis and the CSRs, invited them to lunch, and asked to take over the program. Mavis agreed. The proactive program that Mavis started turned out to be very profitable.

Build Teamwork to Improve Customer Service

Improving teamwork is high on the agenda of most organizations. The reasons for this emphasis are obvious. Without teamwork, everyone—customers, employees and of course the reputation and status of the organization—suffers.

Customers who receive service from your organization know how well your teamwork functions. They know because they benefit when it works well and are hindered when teamwork fails.

Nearly every organization designs a formal customer-support system. The employees involved in this system make up a network of interactive customer support. Each member of the team depends to some degree on other members. When everything works the way it is supposed to, service and support become transparent to the customer. The customer doesn't have to think about service and support factors; they are just there, automatically.

The Informal Support System

Most organizations have installed a formal support system, however, an informal

system continues to thrive. This informal system has been described in many organizations as "how things really get done." In others, however, the informal system functions as a backup when all else fails. The informal system involves employees bypassing the formal structure in order to get the job done.

Regardless of how well either the formal or informal customer-support system functions within your organization, its success is based on the performance and teamwork of you and your coworkers.

The Role of the Frontline Service Person

As a frontline service provider, who has primary contact with customers, your role on the team is greater than the others'. You bear the overall responsibility for satisfying the customer. You have the first contact and the last word with most customers. It is you who must get the support team focused on the customer.

If the system breaks down and delivers poor service, the customer normally blames you and expects you to fix the situation. Probably few, if any, of the team members supporting you have contact with the customer. When they experience problems, they report them to you and in turn expect you to notify the customer. Your plate is full when it comes to teamwork and customer responsibility. You are the unofficial leader of the customer service team.

The Unofficial Leader

The leadership role is not an easy one, especially since it's strictly unofficial. One of your important tasks is to promote teamwork for the benefit of the customer. You are not in a position to order teamwork, but you must, nevertheless, make it work for the customer. As you know, there are different approaches to improving the effectiveness of the customer service team. The approach recommended here is for the leader, the frontline customer service provider, to take certain personal actions that will promote and improve teamwork. Six of the most important actions follow:

Six Personal Actions

1. Be a role model. As the team leader you are constantly being observed and monitored by other team members. The other team members must see that you are committed to customer service and teamwork. By promoting and supporting the service team, you show this dedication. The other team members will watch your behavior and listen for clues on how to act. When you continually talk about customers' needs and expectations and strive to improve service it will be noticed by other team members. In time, they will follow your example. For instance, if you want to improve or change the customer service attitude of the team you must personally display a positive customer service attitude. Being a positive role model is an effective way to promote teamwork.

2. Respect coworkers. It would be great if everyone worked in an environment where they truly liked each other. Sometimes that happens. The important point is, whether you like a coworker or not should have nothing to do with how well you work together. When coworkers work hard and make a contribution they deserve your respect. Offer that respect.

3. Extend trust. Extending trust is an integral part of building teamwork. To have a strong team, trust must be extended from one employee to another. As the customer contact person you have a greater responsibility to make certain the other team members know you trust them.

Most people respond well to responsibility and appreciate it when trust is extended. With responsibility and trust extended from coworkers, greater efforts are made and performance usually improves. Don't be reluctant to depend on other team members and when appropriate ask them to assume certain responsibilities. Extending trust is key to quality teamwork.

4. Listen to others. As the team leader, support players want your ear from time to time. Listen and solicit their ideas on how the support team can be more effective. Furthermore, the more you listen, the more the support coworker will feel like part of the team.

5. Recognition. Have you ever met anyone who didn't like to be recognized for a job well done? Most people appreciate the attention received for a quality performance. As the team leader, much of this recognition responsibility falls on your shoulders. You are the first to know when the customer is satisfied. Share that information by recognizing the team players who contributed to the customer's satisfaction. The recognition need not be a formal announcement. Instead a friendly remark made personally to the individual or in front of other members of the support team will usually meet the requirement.

6. Sharing information. Certain people like to play this game called "I've got a secret." For some reason, they derive strange pleasure—even power—from knowing something others don't. They cling to information that would help team members.

Successful teamwork depends on sharing information. In a changing environment, everyone needs to remain informed. Everyone needs the latest update regarding a customer problem or other situation. If there are new customer policies or procedures, the entire support team needs to know. This is true of any information related to customer-support issues.

Working with the 600-Pound Gorilla

The frontline service person is the unofficial leader of the support team. However, if salespeople are involved, they may have other ideas. On key accounts, a salesperson is normally the team leader. The relationship between service and sales is critical, and far too often there is conflict. Sometimes service feels like a second-class citizen; often sales perceives, "we are out there alone." The conflict between sales and service is much like the standard antagonism often found between staff and the field. What is interesting, however, is the two parties, in both examples, want the same thing— satisfied customers.

These inherent conflicts need to be managed and resolved by the sales and service people involved. The personal actions described in this chapter will help; the salesperson can apply them just as easily as other members of the support team. Sales and service are often in contact with the same customer. Their teamwork, or lack of it, is very obvious to the customer. To resolve the conflict, they need to treat each other as 600-pound gorillas—in other words with great respect.

Conclusion

Teamwork is essential for quality customer service. Frontline service and sales people have special responsibilities to the support team. They are in charge and must provide leadership. This leadership is demonstrated principally by being a strong role model. Use of the personal actions described in this chapter will promote teamwork, and quality teamwork helps satisfy the customer.

Case Study: Focusing the Support Team on the Customer

Jan Miller is the CSR on the Davis Chemical account. She plays her role of sales support and unofficial leader of the support team very well. Over time, she has built strong relationships with her customer contacts at Davis Chemical. In addition, she and the salesperson handling the account, Beverly Brown, work well together.

The needs of the Davis account mean a lot of work and responsibility for Jan. A particular frustration is the difficulty Jan occasionally incurs coordinating services for the account. She says, "It seems there is always someone who resists or throws up a roadblock. They can't expedite, change the schedule or find extra time to meet the customer's needs."

In an attempt to foster more teamwork among her peers on the support team, Jan had a unique idea. Beverly and three of the important customer contacts from Davis Chemical were going to be on-site attending a meeting. Jan and Beverly invited the customers to stay for an extra hour and meet the rest of the support team. The customers accepted, and the meeting was arranged.

Jan invited each member of the support team to attend. By the time she was through, employees from shipping, engineering, clerical support, marketing, mail room, order processing and accounting agreed to attend.

Most of these employees had seldom met customers face to face. They either talked with them on the telephone or usually just heard their name or saw it on labels, shipments and bills.

Jan started the meeting by introducing everyone and explaining his or her responsibility on the Davis account. Next, she asked one of the customers to talk about Davis Chemical and especially how they use the services and products Jan's organization supplies. Several team members asked questions, and a short discussion followed. Jan then asked the

Davis customers why they had selected her company to do business with. The customers talked about the high levels of quality, technology and service they received and the strong relationship they enjoyed with Beverly and Jan. The meeting ended.

In the next few days Jan received several positive comments from her support team. She also noticed a change. The support team was more interested in the Davis account. True, not all the problems magically disappeared, but coordinating services became easier for Jan. Overall service for the customer improved.

Jan accepted her role as unofficial leader of the support team. She found a way to get the team more customer focused. She showed respect for her coworkers by introducing them to the customer and explaining the important role they played. The support team members felt special and realized the impact their jobs had on the customer.

Managing More Telephone Skills

Teaching telephone skills has become a hot topic and may be a mini-industry in itself. There are books, videos, audio cassettes and trainers preaching the correct method of doing this or that. The reason for all this activity is that the telephone skills required to manage a customer conversation are very important.

Technology!

Quality telephone skills today indicate much more than verbal adeptness. You must know and be able to manage voice mail, E-mail, fax, cellular and maybe even computer fax as well as the basic telephone itself. Despite this advanced technology, we still manage to disconnect customers while transferring calls.

You can probably reach your customer, in some fashion, 24 hours a day, 7 days a week. In turn, the customer may have the same access to you. Time frames are compressed as "your machine talks with my machine." While you are commuting to work, a customer leaves a voice mail, assuming you remembered to clear your mailbox. The customer's message is for a

rush order. You arrive, retrieve the message, place the order, call the customer and get her voice mail system. Leave a message stating the order has been placed and the delivery date is next Monday; request a return call if the date is a problem. As you meet briefly with your boss, the customer leaves a voice mail telling you she must have delivery on Friday. You can't reach shipping, so you fax the supervisor and ask him to expedite the order. The supervisor sends you an E-mail confirming the Friday date. You call the customer, only to learn she is out but can be reached in her car. You call her cellular number and confirm the delivery date with the customer, who is speeding down the freeway on her way to an off-site meeting. Whew! Another satisfied customer!

The great thing, as you know, about all these telecommunications systems is they work. They save us time and money and improve our productivity. But they must be managed.

The local telephone company and the long-distance carriers love voice mail. Every call is completed. Every call is a payoff because every call gets connected. It is even connected when your mailbox is full and you're on vacation.

Hide-and-Seek Voice Mail

Some people, perhaps you know a few, receive a large number of calls per day and seldom talk to anyone personally. They have learned to misuse the voice mail system and screen caller messages by seldom directly answering their telephone. Dealing with customers in this manner is poor service.

Customers Want Immediate Service

Whenever possible, the customer deserves and expects the frontline service person to answer. An important customer need is immediate service. The customer's urgency must be dealt with. If the customer contacts your organization with urgent concerns, questions or problems, and constantly gets voice mail and a slow callback, he will not be satisfied. A sign in big letters, for all to see, should be on the wall, stating, **CUSTOMERS WANT A FAST RESPONSE. ANSWER THE PHONE.**

Yours to Manage

The frontline service provider must manage the voice mail system with sensitivity to the customer. Perhaps the volume of

calls prevents you from giving every customer fast service. Even so, don't let customer messages stack up in your mailbox. Retrieve them and call the customers. Also, make certain your personal greeting includes information on how to get immediate service.

When you're not available, let customers know in your personal greeting when they can expect a callback. This allows the customer the choice of waiting for you or requesting immediate service through the alternative you offered.

Another idea is to speak more slowly when leaving your name and telephone number with a customer. Many service providers conclude voice mail messages by repeating their name and telephone number. If the customer missed it in the front part of the message, she won't have to replay the message just to get your name or telephone number.

The Fax and Little Else Is Private

Perhaps you have heard the story of the office sweethearts who left voice mail messages for each other. One day he dialed the voice mail office broadcast code by mistake. The whole office got to listen to him professing his love for her.

It is doubtful many lovers use the fax machine, but it's important to remember it's shared technology in nearly every office. Keep in mind, when sending information, other eyes will probably see your fax.

Perhaps the most public of all is the cellular telephone. When using cellular with a customer, save the confidential information for another time.

All Those Other Skills

If you have been in frontline customer service for very long, you have probably been confronted with telephone-skills

67

training. If it wasn't classroom training, perhaps it was self-training or just closely observing those with more experience. In either case, telephone skills can make or break a frontline service person. They are also crucial to the success of the customer service effort.

Most Frequent Problems

Certain telephone-skill problems never seem to go away. The age-old "let me transfer you" difficulty continues to plague many organizations. Too often the caller is disconnected. The confusion is usually caused by lack of knowledge of how to make the transfer correctly or making a mistake while doing so. Customers get irritated when they are disconnected. It's important to understand how the transfer feature works and to be able to execute it flawlessly.

Another problem that bothers many customers is not knowing to whom they are being transferred. The customer states his request and far too often the response is, "Let me transfer you." Or, worse, the customer hears a click as she is transferred without even being told. As a common courtesy, let the customer know where he is being transferred to. "Please hold on while I transfer you to Joan Smith in Customer Service."

Too often, every call is answered with a "please hold" attached to it. "ABC Bank, please hold." Or "Customer Service, please hold." Some organizations do the "please hold" routine with nearly every caller. The correct and customer-pleasing answer is. "Customer service, will you please hold for a moment?" Next, wait for an answer. Ninety-nine percent of the time customers will say "yes."

More Self-Improvement

The skills described are only a small sampling of the total telephone skills

service providers need to perform their jobs. It is not always easy to be self-critical and "listen to yourself" as you use the various telephone skills associated with your job. But to master these skills you must perform a self-evaluation and then establish an improvement plan. If, for example, you have difficulty with certain behavior on the part of callers, perhaps with angry or demanding customers, include this problem in your self-improvement plan described in chapter 7.

Grade Your Telephone Skills

The following are telephone skills usually associated with customer service. Rate yourself from 1 to 10 on each one to determine if it requires inclusion in your self-improvement plan. There are probably other telephone skills, pertaining to your job, that should also be included. Add them as they come to mind.

TELEPHONE SKILLS FOR CUSTOMER SERVICE	Rating
1. Handling the telephone, including transferring and using "hold"	_____
2. Using voice inflection	_____
3. Answering the customer's call	_____
4. Managing customer objections	_____
5. Negotiating with customers on the telephone	_____
6. The service follow-up call	_____
7. Effective listening	_____
8. Delivering bad news to customers	_____
9. Recognizing and managing customer behavior	_____
10. Closing the conversation	_____

Conclusion

Managing the telecommunication services used in your job requires some thought. Keep in mind that privacy is important to many customers, so be careful with fax, cellular and other less discreet means of communication. Telephone skills are an important part of your job, so understand them well. Include telephone skills in your self-improvement plan.

For an excellent book on telephone skills, read *Telephone Courtesy and Customer Service*. Crisp Publications, Inc.

Case Study: My Voice Mail Talks with Your Voice Mail

The following "customer service" dialogue situation is entirely too common. What do you think of it? Does it sound familiar? Is it quality customer service?

Day One
[Customer calls Stan, his service representative, and gets Stan's voice mail:]

Message: Hi, Stan, this is Barbara. Give me a call.

[Two hours later]

Message: Hi, Barbara, this is Stan returning your call.

[20 minutes later:]

Message: Hi Stan, this is Barbara again. I need to talk to you. The billing statements you sent aren't clear, and I have some questions regarding the brochure. I'll be at my desk for the next hour; then I'll be in a meeting the rest of the day.

[One hour and ten minutes later:]

Message: Hi, Barbara, this is Stan. Sorry I missed you. I went over the statements again, and they are correct. I'll fax you a copy with some notes regarding the changes. That should help you. Call me.

Day Two
Message: Stan, this is Barbara. I looked at the fax you sent, and I still have questions. The brochure situation needs discussing as well. Call me.

[30 minutes later:]

Message: Hi, Barbara. This is Stan returning your call. Call me.

[Five minutes later:]

Message: Stan. This is Barbara. Where did you go so fast? Call me back right away.

[25 minutes later:]

Message: Hi, Barbara, Stan again. Sorry we keep missing each other.

There are rumors, strictly rumors of course, that Stan and Barbara are still trying to talk to each other. When situations like this develop, the customer service provider must take responsibility and become available to the customer. Specifying an exact time to call or be called is one solution. Providing a voice mail procedure so an interruption is possible is another. To continue along the lines of this conversation is a quick way to create an angry customer.

69

You Are Empowered

Writing about customer service without discussing frontline-employee empowerment is difficult. Every organization seems to be trying to empower its employees to perform and make decisions on their own. The old-fashioned American self-reliance principle is being served well. Regardless of what drives empowerment, it's a more productive way to conduct business.

Empowerment Means Balancing Interests

Author/consultant Karl Albrecht, in his book *The Only Thing That Matters*, says "empowerment is responsible freedom." He goes on to say, "When we empower employees, we give them freedom to act responsibly and effectively, not recklessly. We give them the information, knowledge, and skills they need to take responsibility and balance the interests of the customer with the interest of the organization."

The vital message is balance the interests of customer and organization.

Empowerment Is Inherent in American Culture

In American culture, we encourage our children to be independent and self-reliant. Even so, conflict often arises between parent and child when the child reaches for independence. The child, in an autonomous action, makes a decision of which the parent doesn't approve, and there is conflict. The child says, "I was doing what you wanted, making my own decisions." The parent replies, "But you didn't use good judgment."

The Empowerment Struggle

In the workplace, both employees and management often struggle in similar fashion to the family. Empowerment can mean conflicts between employees and management, as both err in trying to make the empowerment process work.

In customer-focused organizations, balancing these interests is much less of an issue. The reason? The entire operation understands that satisfying customer needs is in its best interest. In other words, the interests of the customer are the interests of the organization. However, conflict happens when there are different interpretations of customer needs and organizational interests among frontline personnel, support groups and other departments. In this environment, frontline service employees face the issue of trying to do what is best for the customer—only to sometimes find themselves in discord with support units. Often they feel customers pushing from one side while their organization pushes back from the other. Because they take both customer and organizational responsibilities seriously, they frequently perceive themselves as caught in the middle.

Advocate: One Who Pleads or Argues on Behalf of Another

When work units of the organization are not 100 percent customer focused, frontline personnel must become the customer's advocate. They represent the customer's interests and, in turn, protect the organization from losing a customer. Everyone wins!

Example 1.

The engineering group changes the customer's delivery date because of design problems. The customer will have no work for five employees for 30 days because of this decision. Someone must act as the customer's advocate.

In some organizations, especially large ones, it is not uncommon to have a policy clearly proclaiming sales and frontline service as the customer's advocates. They are charged with representing the customer's needs to the rest of the organization.

Example 2.

For the second consecutive month, the customer's bill is wrong. The customer says she won't pay the bill until it's corrected. Accounting tells the customer go ahead and pay, and the next bill will show the correction. The customer says no. Accounting sends an overdue notice to the customer. The customer threatens to cancel the account.

Someone must act as the customer's advocate.

Empowerment Doesn't Always Mean Renting a Plane

We have all heard the story, or one similar to it, about the employee who learned

71

a Christmas shipment was delayed because of a storm. Knowing many customers would be dissatisfied, the employee decided to charter an airplane to deliver the packages.

As a frontline customer service provider, do you have the authority to charter a plane? Would it be good judgment on your part?

Being empowered doesn't mean you will ever have to rent an airplane or execute some other deed of notoriety in order to satisfy a customer. More realistically, it means providing quality service on an everyday basis. Service that satisfies the customer.

How Much Authority Do You Have, Anyway?

Granting authority to provide customer service is one of the first steps toward quality service. In American business, the way this authority is handed off to frontline employees is interesting. While many organizations struggle to find the right words to form the perfect empowerment mission statement, others use little formal written information to convey the empowerment message, and are service leaders.

Case in Point: Nordstrom

Stories of outstanding service by empowered employees are common at Nordstrom. Perhaps the most famous is the story of the customer who returned an automobile tire. Of course, Nordstrom is a very successful specialty retailer featuring clothing and accessories. The store has never carried tires or similar merchandise.

Nordstrom had recently taken over space previously occupied by a store that did sell tires. The customer was confused and insisted the tire had been purchased from Nordstrom. The salesperson put the customer first and accepted the tire. Obviously, the salesperson was empowered to do so.

The customer comes first. Cheryl Engstrom, Nordstrom Corporate Media Relations Manager, verified this tire story. She went on to explain that organizationally, Nordstrom operates from an inverted-pyramid style of management. The customer comes first, followed by sales and sales-support people, then managers and buyers, and finally the board of directors. She further added, "Our salespeople answer to their customers first, rather than to a manager when making decisions about how to satisfy customers."

A personnel-department brochure at Nordstrom states, "We encourage our salespeople to be innovative in their sales techniques. There is no set method or procedure manual of specific selling practices. Employees are simply asked to use good judgment."

Empowerment Comes with the Job

As a frontline service provider, you are automatically empowered to satisfy customer needs. It comes with the job. The only thing that may be undecided is the scope of your empowerment. In some cases your "good judgment" may be the limit to your empowerment. If your scope of empowerment is unclear, there are still a great many actions you can undertake to ensure customer satisfaction. Fifteen of those actions are listed below.

Fifteen Personal Actions of Self-Empowerment
1. Be the customer's advocate by representing his or her interest to your organization.

2. Explore every alternative before saying "no."

3. Strive to balance the customer's interests with your organization's interests.

4. Do your part to make the customer's and your organization's interest one and the same.

5. Work closely and effectively with support units by understanding their point of view, while continually emphasizing customer needs.

6. Promote teamwork in order to help support customer service.

7. Give the customer the benefit of the doubt.

8. Avoid becoming so customer focused that you lose sight of your organization's best interests.

9. When appropriate, work to get support personnel face to face with customers.

10. Agree with sales on account responsibility. Honor the agreement.

11. Work to make your organization a customer-focused one.

12. Be realistic about your customer service. Find ways to make it even stronger.

13. Show others how effectively empowerment works.

14. Continue to work to understand customer needs fully.

15. Keep in mind that successful empowerment consists more of day-to-day perseverance than renting airplanes and taking back a tire.

Conclusion

You are empowered to satisfy customer needs by balancing the customer's interest with those of your organization. Inherent in your job is the empowerment to take a wide range of actions that will meet customer needs.

Case Study: Good Judgment Is a Must

John was viewed as a good frontline service provider. However, his supervisor felt John had one fault: occasionally he failed to use good judgment. During John's performance review, the supervisor cited an incident where John's good judgment was, as the supervisor put it, "less than desired."

The situation the supervisor referred to was as follows:

The Situation

John dispatches technicians as part of his job. Customers call with a system problem, and John determines if a technician is needed at the customer's location. Sandy, from American Distribution, called late one afternoon and complained that her company's system wasn't running correctly. John discussed the problem with Sandy and determined a technician would have to go out. John's problem was all the technicians were assigned to other customers; in addition, the workday was about to end. John asked Sandy if he could send someone in the morning. Sandy said no, insisting a technician be sent immediately. John explained to Sandy that her system problem wasn't very serious and could be fixed within a few minutes the next morning. Again, Sandy insisted someone come out.

John found an available technician and dispatched her on an overtime basis to American Distribution. The technician fixed the problem shortly after arriving,

73

but got stuck in heavy traffic upon returning and charged a total of three hours of costly overtime.

The Conflict

Supervisor: John, dispatching the technician was unnecessary. You know that the problem was a nonemergency and should have been handled the next morning. American Distribution is a small account, and we can't afford to spend costly overtime resources unless it's absolutely necessary.

John: I knew it wasn't an emergency, but the customer insisted on same-day service. The bottom line is customer satisfaction, and all I was trying to do was put the customer first.

Supervisor: John, your *first* responsibility was to convince the customer that her problem wasn't serious and could wait until the next morning.

Who's Right?

You be the judge. Is the supervisor correct in criticizing John's action? Did John make good judgments in handling the customer's problem? Did John balance the customer's need with his organization's need?

When frontline people are managing multiple calls per day and involved in countless other activities, mistakes happen. Few organizations expect perfection. However, empowerment means extending trust to an employee and that trust includes an expectation of good judgment. Good judgment is not optional; it is a responsibility.

Satisfying the Existing Customer

Customers already in your base are different from those making occasional inquiries. They are the reason you have a job, and they provide the revenue to keep your organization going. In short, the satisfaction of the existing customer is of the utmost importance to everyone in your organization.

Earlier in this book, gaining a customer was portrayed as a sort of capturing process: A customer becomes dissatisfied, and another organization captures him. Or a new customer contacts you, and with a strong service effort, you capture her.

Indeed, you must try to capture new customers, but don't take the existing ones for granted. Too often, the service effort and emphasis extended toward gaining a new customer is stronger than what the existing customer receives.

All service providers need to remind themselves that long-term customers are free to leave at any time.

Benefits of Long-Term Customers

An important benefit to maintaining your existing customers is that their satisfaction will attract new customers. First, satisfied customers refer their associates to your organization. Second, a satisfied customer base enhances your reputation, which attracts new customers to your organization.

The Never-Ending Capturing Process

We think of capturing a customer as a singular event—that is, the day the customer decides to conduct business with our organization. However, providing quality service includes recapturing the existing customer each time you are in contact. When you do this successfully and repeatedly, the customer becomes comfortable and satisfied with the relationship.

The Predictable Customer

Customers are somewhat predictable: As long as they are comfortable and satisfied, they will not leave. Customer comfort can be defined in different ways, but basically it means that customer needs are met. This includes service, price, quality and a host of other factors from which customers derive satisfaction.

Let's explore this idea of customer comfort, because it is a critical customer need.

The Grocery Store

For a lasting relationship to work, customers must feel comfortable where and with whom they conduct business. Think, for example, about where you shop for groceries. You probably go to a store that is convenient to work or home and that has fair prices. If you have shopped at this particular store for very long, you are most likely very comfortable doing so. As a rule, we don't do business for very long where we are not comfortable. The reasons for your comfort with your personal grocery store relates to a variety of factors, as does your customers' relationship with you. To illustrate the point, take a moment to complete the following exercise.

THE GROCERY STORE CASE

QUESTION: I am comfortable shopping at my grocery store because: (Rate each reason on a 1 to 10 scale. One is poor and 10 is excellent.)

REASON	SCALE
Convenience	1 2 3 4 5 6 7 8 9 10
Prices	1 2 3 4 5 6 7 8 9 10
Service	1 2 3 4 5 6 7 8 9 10
Easy to Do Business With	1 2 3 4 5 6 7 8 9 10
Product Selection	1 2 3 4 5 6 7 8 9 10
Quality of Products	1 2 3 4 5 6 7 8 9 10
Friendly Employees	1 2 3 4 5 6 7 8 9 10
Cleanliness	1 2 3 4 5 6 7 8 9 10
Easy Parking	1 2 3 4 5 6 7 8 9 10
Overall Value	1 2 3 4 5 6 7 8 9 10
Other Reasons	
_____	1 2 3 4 5 6 7 8 9 10
_____	1 2 3 4 5 6 7 8 9 10

Now, select the three reasons with the highest comfort scores. Suppose you changed the rating of these top three to a 5. Would you continue to feel as comfortable with the store? Probably not. Would you find another grocery store in which to do your shopping, or at least start thinking about doing so? Yes, you probably would.

Customers Don't Always Compain; They Just Leave

You would also do what your own customers do when they don't get what they want—complain very little or not at all. Customers of a grocery store or of any organization generally do not like to complain. If they become dissatisfied, they typically just move on or at least start thinking about finding a new place to conduct business and receive service. To keep customers, you have to ensure they are continually comfortable.

What Makes Customers Comfortable?

Understanding why customers are comfortable conducting business with you requires knowing what they want. For example, can your customer get nearly equal products or services at similar prices from a competitor? If so, then the customer has selected you because of service and support.

Customers do business with organizations that they rate highly in:

- Services

- Products

- Support

- Costs

If the customer's comfort level is strong in all four categories, the overall value will be highly rated. Of course, the personal relationship between you and the customer is important. When this relationship is strong, the customer often is willing to overlook other "less satisfying" factors.

Service and Support: The Job of Frontline

As a frontline service provider, you control much of the service and support provided the customer. Your responsibility is considerable. It is you who must make customers comfortable by first understanding what they want and then providing as much of that "want" as possible. Let's discuss what customers want.

The Laundry-List Approach
The following is what can best be described as a laundry list of customers' wants. Your job is to rate (1 to 10) each customer want just as you did with the grocery store example. This time, however, you are rating each item as you think your customer would rate it.

CUSTOMER SERVICE WANTS

Customers want service that is:

SERVICE	SCALE
Hassle Free	1 2 3 4 5 6 7 8 9 10
Courteous	1 2 3 4 5 6 7 8 9 10
Reliable	1 2 3 4 5 6 7 8 9 10
Flexible	1 2 3 4 5 6 7 8 9 10
Fast	1 2 3 4 5 6 7 8 9 10
Accurate	1 2 3 4 5 6 7 8 9 10
Value added	1 2 3 4 5 6 7 8 9 10
Friendly	1 2 3 4 5 6 7 8 9 10
Consistent	1 2 3 4 5 6 7 8 9 10
Trustworthy	1 2 3 4 5 6 7 8 9 10
Knowledgeable	1 2 3 4 5 6 7 8 9 10
Helpful	1 2 3 4 5 6 7 8 9 10
Responsive	1 2 3 4 5 6 7 8 9 10
Advice Provided	1 2 3 4 5 6 7 8 9 10
Personal	1 2 3 4 5 6 7 8 9 10

Add and rate other wants your customers may have.

_____ 1 2 3 4 5 6 7 8 9 10
_____ 1 2 3 4 5 6 7 8 9 10

Customers Expect a Lot
You probably have high ratings on most of the items listed. As you know, customers want and usually expect a lot. As customers, they are entitled to do so. Suppose you asked each of your existing customers personally to rate his wants on a 1 to 10 scale, just as you have done. Now imagine just before you talk or meet with an existing customer you review her ratings and respond accordingly. Would you have a better idea of how to protect your customer base and to make the customer comfortable? Sure you would. Would the rating make it easier to satisfy customers? Of course it would.

Take the Mystery Out of What Customers Want
To have an individual "wants" rating sheet in front of you for each customer is not

too practical. However, you can make a safe assumption: Assume your customers rated nearly all of their wants as a 10. Now the mystery has been removed. You know what your customers want.

Conclusion

The new, uncaptured customer is important. But the existing customer is the lifeblood of the organization. Understanding what this customer wants and what makes her comfortable is the key to a long, profitable relationship. Keeping a customer captured with quality service applies to the existing customer as well as the potential customer. It is a never-ending process.

Case Study: Determining If the Existing Customer Is Satisfied

Tyler is a strong customer service provider who is very interested in a sales career with his organization, Endicott Insurance Company. He currently services 75 accounts. These accounts talk with Tyler regarding inquiries ranging from claims questions to policy explanations. Usually Tyler is pretty busy, but lately the calls have slowed. He decides

this is his chance to demonstrate his sales skills. He tells the manager, "I have some time right now. Suppose I do some cold-calling and see how many leads I can generate?" "I have a better idea," the manager replies. "Call the last 25 accounts you provided service to and ask two questions. First, ask if they are satisfied with the response they received to their inquiry. Second, ask if there is anything else you can do for them."

Without much enthusiasm, Tyler started calling. Within a couple of hours he had plenty of work. He learned many of his accounts still had questions or concerns that generally stemmed from their previous conversation with him. In fact, one account was thinking about canceling its policy because of confusion regarding a claim. Tyler was able to save the account.

Later, the manager explained his thoughts to Tyler. "Insurance is complicated for most people, and it's easy to have a misunderstanding. Therefore, it doesn't take much to lose a customer."

In short, Tyler recaptured an existing customer while providing quality service to others. Not a bad day's work.

Measuring Service Performance

Nearly every customer service organization has a job-performance-measuring system of some sort. Normally, two factors are measured; the customer's satisfaction, and the individual performance of the customer service employee. Employee performance is measured in a wide variety of ways. Depending on the size of the organization, an extensive performance review may be administered by a supervisor or manager at particular intervals during the year. If the organization is less formal or smaller, the review may never make it onto paper and instead be an ongoing verbal process. More than likely your performance is measured, at least in part, with quantitative information often called values or objectives. For example, the number of calls you manage per day, the number of different types of customers you contact, the amount of time you spend with each customer, the revenue you produce, the feedback you receive from customer surveys, the orders you write...and generally more numbers and then more numbers.

Measuring Customer Satisfaction

Part of the reason for all this number crunching is to attempt to measure the effectiveness of the customer service provider. Such quantitative information does have value, but it tells only a small portion of the story. The real story is told in terms of customer satisfaction. Is the customer satisfied? To what degree? These are questions that should be ever present in all customer service groups. Far too often, we fail to get our arms around the true customer service picture and simply use numbers to declare the customer satisfied. When this is done, we eventually learn the real truth, which often differs from our perception.

Who Measures Customer Service?

There was a time (older people like that phrase) when management alone measured service. Today, all the participants of the customer service group should share in the measurement of service; an important role is reserved for the frontline service provider. Frontline is where the information regarding levels of customer satisfaction exists. With daily customer contact, frontline is in a position to know if the customer is satisfied. There is, of course, a catch. The frontline person needs to understand what customers want and to possess enough experience to recognize when a customer is dissatisfied. Perhaps most important, frontline needs to be objective.

Objectivity Is the Hard Part

To be objective means not to be influenced by emotion or personal prejudices and not to hide from the truth. When a service provider has spent a great deal of energy and time in an attempt to satisfy a customer, it is very difficult to accept that the customer may not be satisfied. Human nature rebels against admitting that we failed to satisfy the customer when we put forth a strong effort. But that is exactly what we must do. Conversely, when the customer is satisfied, we need to take credit, and patting ourselves on the back is certainly acceptable. When the service provider can be objective, is experienced and understands what customers want, he is in a position to evaluate his own performance.

How Frontline Can Measure Customer Satisfaction

Marcy finished a long conversation with a customer. She thought the contact was difficult. The customer had had many questions and wanted more in-depth information than usual. The conversation had ended with the customer saying he had the needed information and would call Marcy back.

Marcy took a minute to evaluate how she had managed the conversation and to determine the level of customer satisfaction. She used the following five questions to make her evaluation.

Five Key Questions

1. Did I completely understand what the customer wanted?

2. Did the customer get what he/she wanted?

3. Did I present the information in a clear and concise matter?

4. Did the customer receive quality service?

5. Is the customer satisfied?

When answered, these five basic questions tell the story of most customer contacts. Following each conversation with a customer, frontline service people need to ask themselves these questions. Use the questions consistently in order to ensure customer satisfaction and to measure the service performance. Normally, little thought is given to most customer contacts unless there is some doubt about the customer's satisfaction or there is a known problem. The five questions, when answered objectively, provide valuable insight to service performance.

Time Adds Perspective

An effective added measurement is to repeat the five questions after a few hours have passed. Objectivity often increases with time. Most readers will recall reviewing a work situation while relaxing at home. Some of us have been known to do it every day. You replay the events and what was said, and suddenly you have a different perspective of the situation. Reviewing situations and conversations with customers is critical if quality service is the goal. The review process allows for self-measurement and provides the basis for improvement. Determine what areas need improvement, and then apply the steps from chapter 7 on self-improvement.

Exploring the Five Questions

Let's take a moment to examine the five questions and determine what should be considered as part of the answers.

Question 1: Did I Completely Understand What the Customer Wanted?

A customer request for service usually includes a clearly stated "want." An obvious example is when the customer says, "I want to order ten of your new widgets." At other times, what the customer wants is not expressly stated, but comes out during the conversation. For example, suppose a customer asks you to go over her bill. While explaining the bill, you learn the customer has difficulty in understanding the billing format. Therefore, the customer's want becomes (1) an easier-to-understand bill format and/or (2) information on how to read and understand the bill. When answering question 1, you need to consider both the stated and unstated customer wants.

Question 2: Did the Customer Get What He/She Wanted?

Because the service provider responds to the inquiry and makes every effort to satisfy the customer, he is prone to answer "yes" to question 2. The correct answer requires objectivity on the part of the frontline service provider. Did the customer *really* get what he wanted? Or do we *wish* and *hope* he got what he wanted? It is easy to rationalize the situation. This question requires honesty because it's at the core of customer service: Customers who get what they want are satisfied and those who don't are less satisfied.

Question 3: Did I Present the Information in a Clear and Concise Manner?

When presenting information, gaining customer concurrence as you proceed is essential. There is little point in holding off the customer while you present the information. When the customer is commenting, asking and answering questions, and discussing key points, it is a sign everything is clear because each issue or question is discussed and answered as you proceed. As a double check, for courtesy and when appropriate, ask the customer if everything is clear, and if she is satisfied with the information you imparted.

Question 4: Did the Customer Receive Quality Service?

Answering this question also requires objectivity, along with some insight and positive answers to the previous questions. Quality service is in the eye of the customer, and the customer is the final judge of the service effort. If the answers to the first three questions are positive, then it is likely the response to this one will be positive as well. When answering the quality-service question, the service provider needs to keep in mind whether the customer is receiving what he wants in a timely and acceptable manner. Of course, when appropriate, you can ask the customer. For example:

"I know we covered a lot, but I hope you are satisfied with everything. Is that the case?"

"How satisfied are you with the service you received?"

"Our goal is to provide quality service. How do you feel we did?"

"On a scale of 1 to 10, how would you rate the service you received?"

"What more could we have done?"

Question 5: Is the Customer Satisfied?

Again, if the previous questions are answered positively, then the customer is probably satisfied. Sometimes, frontline service people get the idea the customer must have everything he wants in order to be satisfied. That is usually not the case. There are acceptable alternatives to most customer wants, and when the choice is stated in terms of benefits to the customer, the customer will respond in a positive manner. Remember, most customers appreciate receiving advice when it's appropriate. So when a customer states a want and frontline service can't satisfy it, perhaps it's time to be creative and find an alternative solution that will satisfy the customer just as much.

Conclusion

Responsibility for measuring customer service is spread throughout the service organization. However, the frontline service provider has a key role. Ideally, following each customer contact the service provider will ask the five questions outlined in this chapter to try to determine the satisfaction level of the customer. In this deliberate and analytical way, service can be measured on a contact-by-contact basis, and areas that need improvement can be self-identified. The accuracy of this measurement approach depends very much on the objectivity of frontline service personnel. When frontline sincerely desires quality service, objectivity is just one more factor to manage.

Case Study: The Feedback System

Dan supervised a small group of customer-support employees at Royal Manufacturing, Inc., a company that produced bicycles. The company featured an 800 number for retailers, customers and anyone else with a question about Royal bicycles. Dan's group managed hundreds of inquiries each day. The inquiries consisted of requests for information about the nearest retailers, parts, bicycle operation and warranties, and questions about bicycle repair.

As part of Royal's quality-service program, each customer who called received a brief questionnaire in the mail about her service experience and satisfaction with the 800 number. Dan and his group were interested in seeing how their perception of the service they provided tracked with what the customers thought. To do this, they decided to measure their service more closely for a five-day period.

The employees, using the five questions, rated each call. Every day the ratings were handed in on an anonymous basis. Dan analyzed the results and concluded the group members felt they provided a quality effort resulting in very good service. Only a handful of ratings indicated the employees thought the service they provided needed improvement, didn't meet the company's quality standards or simply could not satisfy the customer.

After two weeks, the customers' questionnaires came in. Nearly 15 percent of the customers responded to the survey. The 15 percent was a large sample and certainly representative of the whole.

The customer feedback was favorable except for the final survey question. The question was, "Did you receive quality service?" Seventy-seven percent of the respondents answered "yes." Eight percent didn't respond to the question, and 15 percent answered "no."

What Do You Think?

Does Dan's group have a serious problem?

Do the employees need to improve their objectivity?

Do further efforts need to be made to determine why 15 percent said they didn't receive quality service?

One Answer

When 15 percent of the customers indicate they didn't receive quality service, it's a serious problem. An important factor is the trend of the results. Is this 15 percent on its way to 20 percent or is it headed towards 10 percent? Measuring the trend can be done by comparing customer responses over time.

The objectivity of the employees was actually better than average. Their perception of their service was closer than most employees generally are, and they correctly identified a small percentage of dissatisfied customers before the survey. A lot of organizations would like to have 77 percent of their customers state they received quality service. Obviously, the reasons 15 percent are not receiving quality service should be explored. The answers need to be found and can be, given enough research.

The Basic Actions of Customer Service

If you start talking about basic actions that help satisfy customers in front of service employees or salespeople, you hear one thing: "We already know that." Of course they know it, especially when they see it or hear it. But the need for frontline service employees to constantly review and practice the basic techniques, that are proven to be customer satisfying, is key to the success of the service organization. Highly skilled customer service providers spontaneously use these basic techniques along with others to ensure customer satisfaction. But regardless of the skill level, all service providers occasionally need to review the basic techniques that lead to quality service.

In this chapter we will examine five of the techniques every frontline employee should know. These five have been selected because they offer skills and suggestions required to meet everyday recurring situations frontline service encounters.

Technique One: Managing the Angry Customer

Customers come at frontline with all forms of behavior. Sometimes they are

angry, hurried, passive, demanding, rude, friendly, talkative and a host of other behaviors. Each behavior is distinct and requires an individual response. From time to time, nearly every frontline service provider is faced with an angry customer. So let's review a few ideas on how to manage a conversation with an angry customer.

The angry customer is a challenge for most customer service providers. Experienced frontline people accept this challenge and strive to manage the conversation just as they do with any other customer. Calming an angry customer and then meeting the customer's needs is a satisfying experience. A few guidelines apply to every angry-customer situation.

Don't Get in the Swamp with the Alligator

Anger is an emotional response to a particular circumstance. The actual anger may be deep rooted and often is caused by something other than what the customer is complaining about.

Dan West was having a terrible day. He had car trouble while driving to work. His boss expressed her dissatisfaction regarding some recent results. One of Dan's subordinates called in sick, so Dan was trying to fill in for him and do his own job as well. Then Dan learns that his computer paper order has been delayed until Friday. He calls and expresses extreme anger over the delay.

In this example, what is Dan angry about? The delayed order? His car? His boss? His workload? Probably all of the above. But regardless of the reason, the frontline representative is going to feel the brunt of Dan's anger. When customers express anger it is often an emotional display. Frontline personnel should view the emotion, the heat of the moment, as the "swamp." The customer service representative must avoid this swamp. In other words, don't get involved in the customer's emotion. Two angry people attempting conversation usually accomplishes little.

To Find a Solution, Someone Has to Be Rational

When the customer is emotional, frontline service must be rational and calm in order to solve the customer's problem. Experienced frontline people know they must first understand the problem and,

when appropriate, determine the cause. Only by remaining detached from the emotion of the moment can the solution process begin to take place.

The Customer Needs Assurance

When a customer has a problem and is angry, he needs to hear assuring words that his reason for the anger is understood and something will be done about it. Let's look at a typical response that provides assurance. Dan West calls and is very angry over his delayed order.

> **Dan:** I *must* have that order today. As much buiness as we give you, there's no excuse....
>
> **Frontline:** Mr. West, I understand why you are upset. I need to determine how we can improve the date. It will take a few minutes. Let me call you back within 15 minutes, and I will have an answer for you. Will that be all right?

Let's quickly review what frontline accomplished in the response to Dan West.

1. He was told his anger was understood.

2. He received assurance that something would be done.

3. He was presented with an action plan.

Is Dan West satisfied? He still has the same problem, but now at least he knows something is going to be done.

The Angry Customer Needs to Hear the Right Words

So far Dan West has received assurance. During moments of anger or just ordinary concern, customers need to hear assuring words—words that say a solution or an answer will be provided. This doesn't mean the customer will be ultimately satisfied with the final feedback from frontline. Sometimes there isn't any "good news" for the customer. But even bad news needs to be presented professionally and with assurance that every effort will be made in the future to avoid a recurrence of the problem or situation.

Let's look at a "bad news" professional reply to Dan West and the ensuing conversation.

> **Frontline:** Mr. West, I checked on your order, and unfortunately we aren't able to improve the date. However, I did confirm that you will receive the paper on Friday.

> **Dan West:** I don't understand. I placed that order in plenty of time for a Tuesday delivery.

> **Frontline:** I know you did. In fact, as you know, we rarely miss our promised delivery dates. But this was an unavoidable situation. I talked with the factory to see if there was any way we could deliver early, but Friday is the best date we can provide. Again, I apologize for the delay and want to assure you that in the future you can expect us to meet our promised dates.

The conversation probably goes on for another minute or so. Note that frontline did not offer an excuse for the delay. Earlier we discussed not sharing internal problems with customers. In the case of a dissatisfied customer, it becomes an individual judgement whether to share the cause of the problem with the customer. In the Dan West situation, stating "The factory has a large workload and our shipments have been delayed" will only exacerbate the customer's anger. If the customer asks or insists on an answer, then provide one, but initially avoid sharing internal problems.

Technique Two: Provide Basic Courtesy

Frontline people get busy—they're swamped with calls, callbacks, problems, customers waiting, delays, frustration and on most days a wide range of demanding and rewarding work. In this hectic environment it's sometimes easy to forget about common courtesy. Let's quickly look at five important guidelines related to consistently offering courtesy to customers.

1. Always greet the customer and then offer to help.

   > "Good morning, Mr. West. How may I help you?"
   > "Good afternoon, Ms. West. How are you today?"
   > "What can I do for you?"

2. Constantly use the language of courtesy.

   > "Thank you." "You're welcome."
   > "Thanks for your business."
   > "I enjoyed talking with you." "Thanks for calling."
   > "We appreciate your business. Thanks again."
   > "Feel free to call anytime."
   > "Would you like to hold or shall I call you right back?"

3. Speak in positive, action-oriented terms.

   > "I will call you before three o'clock."
   > "The shipment will arrive on Friday."
   > "I'll send the information immediately."
   > "It will be in the mail this afternoon."
   > "I'll call and double check for you."
   > "I will be glad to take care of that for you."

4. Keep the customer informed.

   > "If there is a problem of any sort, I'll call you back."
   > "I wanted to let you know the paperwork is complete."
   > "You will have the material by Friday."
   > "The minute I get the new date I'll call you."
   > "The meeting time has been changed to one o'clock."

5. Use common sense.

> Keep telephone customer hold time to a minimum.
> Answer the telephone within three rings.
> Make yourself available to the customer.
> Assume the customer is right.
> Listen and then listen some more.
> Be attentive.

Technique Three: Meeting Commitments

Customers are promised nearly everything in the course of a business day. They hear: "The check is in the mail." "I'll call you right back." "You will have all the material before the meeting." "The technician is on her way." "The brochure will arrive on Thursday." Customers have learned they simply can't depend on certain people and organizations. When they learn this hard truth they avoid the situation and find organizations that can be trusted to do business with. If you want your customers to stay captured, make sure to keep your commitments made to them.

Control Your Optimistic Self

Everyone likes to be optimistic and give the customer "good news." Frontline service providers are very concerned about their customers and want to satisfy them. The last thing they want is to disappoint their customers. But there are times when the bad news has to be delivered: "The date can't be met." "The special material is more expensive than we originally quoted." "The box of widgets is really on a truck in the middle of a snowstorm."

The Temptation

The temptation all frontline employees face is to save face and put a positive spin on bad news. Customers hear such words as:

> "It looks like we may have a problem delivering everything on Friday. However, I'm still working on it. I should have an answer this afternoon."

When in fact the reply should be:

> "I'm sorry, but we will not be able to deliver on Friday."

Customer Expectation

Customers want the truth. They too are business people and understand not everything goes smoothly all the time. Customers expect frontline to do everything possible to meet their promises, but they are realistic and know there will be occasional delays or other problems even in the best of organizations. However, customers do expect consistency. They will usually tolerate a few problems, but certainly not on a consistent basis.

Technique Four: Avoid Complacency

Avoiding complacency is much more a state of mind or, perhaps, an attitude than it is a technique. It is worth discussing, however, because it is so important to the success of any service organization. Customer service providers, like all employees and managers, have been known to accept things as they are; to slow the drive for even better service; to just slide through a particular day without extending a maximum service effort. They assume the customer is satisfied when reality says she's not.

The frontline service job is a tough one, and it's only natural to sit back at times, be a little complacent and get some relief from the calls; the large numbers of customers, and all the associated problems.

There Is No Room for Complacency

Despite the pressure for high-service performance, there is no acceptable rationalization for being complacent. The quality-service effort is a never-ending process. Complacency kills quality service faster than anything else. One of the most dangerous periods in the life of a frontline service organization is when everyone agrees, "The customers are satisfied and everything is just fine." Because providing service is dynamic and the competitor is poised to capture, there simply is no room for complacency.

Technique Five: Listening to the Customer

The next time you are in the library, look at the number of books that include the subject of listening. You may be surprised by the volume. Listening is a topic that continues to grow in importance. Why? Because customer relationships are critical, and at their core is communication. Communication means the exchange of thoughts, messages or information. None of this can be done without listening. Listening, in a frontline service environment, is sometimes described as 50 percent of customer communication. It is, in fact, much more—perhaps as high as 80 percent. Observe a skilled customer

service representative and notice how she listens to the customer. She typically asks questions, offers short explanations, provides assurance and confirms what the customer has said. She avoids monologues and unnecessary conversation. She is businesslike, to the point and she listens to what the customer is saying and responds accordingly.

The Difficulty of Listening
The business and customer problems caused by poor listening are enormous. The reason? Listening is one of the most difficult skills of the service provider's job. For many it is the hardest skill to master.

And in This Corner, Adding to the Listening Difficulty...
The difficulty of listening, especially in a service situation, is compounded by the need to respond to what is heard. The requirement to respond means that, while listening intently to the customer, a response must be organized and stated in a word description the customer will understand. Of course, this customer response should also be offered, whenever possible, in terms of benefit to the cutomer. No small task!

Listening Can Be a Dual Problem
Of course, the listening problem exists on both sides of the communication fence. Customers, like all of us, can fail to tune in to what is being said just as quickly as frontline can. The difference is, it's the responsibility of frontline to listen to and understand the customer. Frontline service providers are responsible for effective communication with customers, and when the customer doesn't understand it's the service provider's fault.

Being an effective customer service provider means listening, formulating and delivering an effective response and taking responsibility for the customer's understanding of the communication.

A 10-Step Plan to Improve Listening Skills

Frontline customer-contact employees should use any or all of the following ten suggestions to improve listening skills.

1. Remain aware of the importance of listening.

2. When talking with customers, focus on each word.

3. Make notes as the conversation progresses. Write down key words or concepts.

4. When needed or appropriate, replay the customer's words for confirmation.

5. Listen for customer conversational tone, inflection, and any undercurrent that might be a clue to customer attitude.

6. Shut out other noise and conversations by pressing the telephone receiver closer to your ear or closing your eyes. (Yes, it works!)

7. Don't anticipate what the customer is going to say. This applies even when it is absolutely clear what the customer is about to say. Hear the words for the first time.

8. Stop other activities when listening on the telephone. Don't continue to read or search for papers, pens or other temporarily misplaced materials.

9. Avoid side conversations when on the telephone.

10. Constantly review your listening skills. Ask yourself, how often is

there confusion between you and a customer over what was said? How often do you have to call a customer back in order to clarify something previously discussed?

Conclusion

The five techniques presented in this chapter are a partial list of the skills that customer service providers need. The five are at the top of the list. Every service person should strive to master them. Successfully managing conversations with angry customers is a skill all need to know. Basic courtesy is part of every face-to-face or telephone meeting. When commitments are consistently met, customers tend to perceive the service as excellent. Complacency must be avoided. Finally, listening skills are at the very core of quality service. These five actions, when mastered, will dramatically improve service and help satisfy customers.

Case Study: Doing Nearly Everything Right

Janet worked for a large regional bank. She prepared loan papers for her internal customer, the loan officer. Janet took pride in her work. She was especially accurate and very careful and thorough regarding details.

In Janet's year-end performance appraisal she received praise for her overall work. However, she was criticized for her frequent failure to meet commitments. Janet replied it was nearly impossible for her to be accurate and still meet all of the deadlines. Janet's supervisor said she understood but the delays were causing the loan officers to miss their commitments to the bank's customers. Therefore, the situation had become serious. The supervisor made it clear that Janet must meet her commitments. Janet's dilemma was how to maintain her high level of accuracy and also meet the loan-officer commitments.

Does This Sound Familiar?

Janet's situation is certainly not unusual. It's very frustrating and somewhat common for an employee to receive a strong performance evaluation with perhaps one exception. Sometimes supervisors and managers have been known to purposely find this "one exception" because of motives known only to them. However, in this case the exception is serious. The customers of the bank are affected. Janet needs an action plan.

Janet's Action Plan

At first, Janet was a little angry and defensive. Her attitude was one that said, "My work is more accurate than anyone's, and the loan officers are too demanding. I guess I'll just be less accurate; then I can meet the deadlines." Janet was a professional, and it didn't take long before she dismissed the negative thoughts and began to concentrate on a plan that would solve the problem. She tried to think of ways to work faster, but felt accuracy would suffer if she did so. The supervisor suggested Janet think about ways to better organize her work.

The supervisor recommended Janet look at each customer file she was working on as a project. Janet caught on immediately. She said, "Then all project activity, file work, is driven by the commitment date to the loan officer." Janet worked out the details and then modified the procedures as she gained experience in her new "project management" work style. Within a short period of time Janet was meeting almost 100 percent of her commitments, and the work load seemed more manageable.

Janet's Choice

Janet was not performing one of the basic actions of customer service very well. She was frequently missing commitments to her internal customer, the loan officer. Janet had a choice: Try to make the changes needed to meet the loan-officer commitments, or accept complacency and let it be "business as usual."

Janet, a professional, would not allow negative thoughts to dominate her. She instinctively knew that she could not be complacent about the situation. Instead, she needed a solution and an action plan. She found both.

Serving the Internal Customer

Many customer service employees provide service and support for internal customers only. A typical example involves employees who perform or coordinate services such as maintenance, clerical support, travel or administrative services in support of internal customers.

Others have the dual role of supporting internal customers and also providing services to external customers. An example is a sales support unit that assists the sales force and also services external customers.

Regardless of the type of support, when one group supports another function or work unit, it is advantageous to think of the supported group as "customers." The mere term "internal customer" helps focus the desired behavior and attitude on the part of those in support positions. The two customers, external and internal, have similar needs that must be satisfied.

More About Internal Customers Who Support External Customers

It seems the further an employee is from the external customer, the less reason he may see to provide unselfish support to the internal customer who does service the outside customer. That is why many organizations find a way to bring this type of employee into direct contact with external customers. Through this contact, the support employee can more readily see the value of supporting the internal customer in order to strengthen the organization's relationship with the external customer. However, as we all know, it is not easy to get an employee to change his focus and accept the internal customer concept. This is especially true in the sales environment.

George schedules the workload of the production planning group. He has responsibility for controlling costs and tries to make as few product design changes as possible.

Salespeople often come to George and ask him to make design changes due to customer needs. George rarely allows changes unless his boss is called and she overrules him. George says he controls costs. Sales says George puts its customers in a position to be captured by the competition.

Gridlock and a constant power struggle characterize this relationship. Sales and George need to resolve the conflict.

Internal Customers Are a Little Different

Internal customers are different from external customers because they come from the same organizational culture as the service provider. There should be a clear understanding of what the internal customer needs. The two groups should be focused on the same end—a successful organization. Even in a small organization, however, multiple face-to-face meetings are usually required to hammer out guidelines and procedures designed to furnish maximum support for whoever carries the title of internal customer. Where the internal customer concept works well, a spirit of cooperation and common purpose can be found.

The Different Attitude

Although the same organizational culture exists between employees who support, and those who have the internal customer role, attitudes can be very different. Imagine a salesperson (internal customer) meeting face to face with a client. The sale hinges on whether the distribution center can deliver three days sooner than normal. The salesperson's attitude says, "We should be able to meet the customer's schedule." The distribution manager's attitude might say, "We can't change our schedule to meet the demands of one customer." In a quality customer-focused organization, strong consideration is given to the salesperson's or service person's perspective, because she is the internal customer and, at the same time, the advocate for the external customer.

The balancing we discussed earlier between the best interests of the organization and the customer's interest strongly come into play in this situation.

This concept of internal customers works well within many organizations, but it is not without its own set of problems and obstacles that must be continually worked on. Let's discuss two of the more prominent situations that arise.

The Second-Class Citizen

The second-class citizen syndrome is one in which the support employee is made to feel or perceives his role as so secondary to his internal customer that he feels slighted or not appreciated. When allowed to develop unchecked, the situation can feed upon itself and cause low morale and related problems for the organization.

This is often a typical feeling in a customer service support-type organization that has contact with external customers but also supports sales or marketing people (internal customers). More than one sales-support employee has cringed as the salespeople go off to the resort to celebrate their sales success and are perceived as having a lofty "air" about them.

How to fix that second class feeling. Fixing the problem is easier said than done. A solution can usually be found if all parties take the responsibility required to correct it.

Management's role. Management needs to be aware of the situation and to consider the feelings and perceptions of the support employee. This awareness should come into play in the planning, directing and controlling phases of the operation. For example, the importance of most external customer jobs means that a recognition program is standard (trips won, etc.). Why not develop one for the support employees? It does not have to be equal in stature or scope, but should recognize the contribution of the internal customer support team and of particular individuals within the team.

The role of the internal customer.
Support people need to know they are
appreciated—they want to feel good about
themselves and their job performance.
Much of this appreciation and recognition needs to come directly from the
internal customer. There are five basic
actions the internal customer can take.

FIVE ACTIONS FOR INTERNAL
CUSTOMERS

1. Make certain the support employees
    understand their importance. Person-
    ally let them know how much they
    are appreciated.

2. Promote and focus teamwork—a team
    concept that includes the support
    person.

3. Keep support employees informed.

4. Take time to listen to their ideas and
    suggestions.

5. Respect the support troops. They work
    hard and deserve your respect, recog-
    nition and appreciation.

The role of internal-customer support.
To be successful, the internal-customer
support employee must recognize that her
role is to support and provide quality
service to the internal customer. That does
mean taking a secodary role. It also means
seeing others receiving more recognition
than is usually offered to support people.
It sort of comes with the territory.

Risk and Reward

Typically, but certainly not always, internal customers take more risks than
support personnel do. Examples are when
the jobs of sales or marketing depend on
revenue produced, when managers must
show quantitative results, when staffers
are responsible for successful planning.

The point is, in our society and within
our business culture we reward those
who take risks and are successful. To
help these people be successful requires
excellent support.

The Importance of Attitude
One of the strongest assets successful
support employees possess is their attitude—an attitude that sees the big picture and the importance of the internal
customer, as well as their own role. An
employee who has an attitude that real-
izes the value of teamwork is key to the
success of the organization.

Conclusion

Conflict between support employees and
internal customers is often inherent
within the organization. It is everyone's
responsibility to resolve conflicts and
find a way to work together successfully.
Management, the internal customer,
and support personnel all share in that
responsibility. However, it is support
who must carry much of the burden for
success. Although they deserve recognition and expressed appreciation, they
often must function effectively without
as much attention as they might like.

The internal-customer concept is a valid
one. Imagine an organization where every
employee viewed coworkers as customers.
Wow! What an organization.

Case Study: Technical Support Employees Change Their Mind

Within high-tech organizations you can
typically find a support group called
Tech Support. This group provides technical support of the end-user customer,
distributor, salesperson or value-added
reseller. Tech support people spend their
day explaining their products and services
and how to use them effectively. They
often help salespeople or resellers build

sales proposals. Tech support is the place nearly everyone turns to get their questions answered and problems solved.

Atlas Computer Services Company was growing, and new salespeople were hired. Of the six new people hired, two came from within the organization and the others from the industry. A few of the Tech Support representatives immediately noticed the four new hires were not as technically proficient as the other Atlas salespeople. They talked about this situation among themselves and generally concluded their company had made a mistake in hiring the four new people. They cited their main reason as "the amount of time we have to spend helping them with sales proposals, other services and product information." The Tech Support reps also knew how well the salespeople were paid, and they began to resent them even more. A very unhealthy situation was developing.

Charlie, a Tech Support rep, noticed the new salespeople were asking him for help considerably more often than the other reps. Charlie had heard the complaints of his coworkers and at first dismissed them as the usual drama. But now he decided to look into the situation. Quietly, he asked two of the new salespeople about their experience with a few of his tech support coworkers. The feedback was not very positive.

Charlie decided to take action. On Monday mornings the Tech Support group had a short meeting. Charlie asked the manager for some time to discuss the issue of support of internal customers.

Charlie began his presentation with a question: "How well are we supporting our internal customers, the salespeople?" The group looked at each other, then back at Charlie. Finally, Nora spoke. She said, "I think there's room for improvement." A group member immediately asked, "What do you mean? "Give me an example." Nora thought for a moment and then said, "I don't think our salespeople are completely satisfied with our performance. Especially our attitude." The group members stirred in their chairs and were about to defend themselves, but Charlie spoke first. "Nora makes a good point and I agree with her."

Don spoke up to defend himself and the others. "Just yesterday I was talking with two of the sales guys, Fred and Maria, and they both indicated how pleased they were with their support."

"How about the new hires? How do you think they feel?" Charlie asked.

Again, the room was quiet for a moment before Don responded to the question. "Have there been any complaints?" he asked.

Charlie replied, "It's not whether there have been complaints that's at issue. The question is whether we're supporting the new hires as well as we can."

The conversation continued for several moments until someone mentioned the lack of knowledge on the part of the new hires. Upon hearing that, Nora offered, "What has their knowledge or lack of it got to do with anything? If they are not as knowledgeable we should provide even more support." Charlie agreed with Nora and pointed out two significant sales that had recently been made by the new hires.

Don replied to Charlie, "I feel like I should get their high salary for as much work as I put into those sales."

Nora bristled when she heard Don's remark. "That's your job," she said. The discussion became heated for a moment, and the salaries of salespeople were mentioned again. Charlie regained control.

He said, "I'm confused. What have the salespeople's salaries got to do with anything?"

Don said, "It's just some of us feel they are paid an awful lot in comparison to what we get."

Mike Cook, the manager, spoke for the first time. "The salespeople are some of the highest-paid employees in our company. They also accept a lot of risk. They produce or they leave, to put it bluntly. In our group our risk is almost nothing in comparison." Mike Cook continued, "As I recall, when sales decided to hire new people I asked if any of you were interested. No one said anything."

The group discussion continued for a few more minutes, and Mike Cook ended it by saying there would be ongoing dialogue about the support issues raised today. He concluded with, "Let's try and deal with facts and not get involved in all the drama about salaries and which salespeople know more. That's simply not our job. This group enjoys a reputation for professionalism. Let's keep it that way."

In the ensuing weeks the group continued to discuss internal-customer support issues. Mike Cook involved the group in designing a survey form for the salespeople to fill out expressing their level of satisfaction. The early survey results were not nearly as positive as the group thought they should be. But with continued focus on the internal customer the surveys improved over time.

What Do You Think?

Was Charlie empowered to do what he did? Would you have taken another course? Was Charlie's approach too direct? Should the manager have been more involved? Should Charlie have involved the manager and let him lead the discussion? Whose responsibility is it to help focus the group on the proper internal-customer behavior—the employee, the manager or both?

Have a Positive Attitude

A good definition of a positive attitude: a helpful state of mind or feeling toward a fact or situation. Simply stated, it is how we perceive things. Perhaps the perfect example is the old glass-of-water illustration. The water in the glass is at the 50 percent mark. Is the glass half full or half empty? A more relevant example is the irate customer. Is he a problem or an opportunity for service? Or how about, Do you feel challenged by the problems you face or let down?

No Quality Without a Positive Attitude

Quality service and a positive attitude go hand in hand. Of all the ingredients required to be a service professional, a positive attitude is the most important. In fact, it is such a strong asset that it can carry a marginal customer service provider. A case in point is a new employee, often with little formal training, who begins a job in customer service. His positive attitude may be a big part of the reason he got the service job in the first place. It is also frequently the reason he survives the early days of managing conversations

with a high volume of customers. In addition, attitude will determine, to a large extent, his degree of long-term success. The power of a positive attitude should never be underestimated. It can be awesome.

The Old Movie Example

In the movie The Bad News Bears, *Walter Matthau played the manager of a disorganized Little League baseball team. The manager and the team have a negative attitude and few playing skills, but eventually find success with new skills and a positive attitude. The transformation the players go through is completely believable for those watching who have a positive attitude. A person with a positive attitude sees opportunities when others do not.*

Sports and the Office

There are countless examples in sports of a team or individual who, despite the odds, wins against a stronger opponent. Although less publicized, the same thing happens in customer service organizations every day. For example:

- The irate customer who threatens to cancel her account, but instead places an order as a result of the way the problem was managed.

- The important customer who was captured because she received outstanding service.

Of course, the best model is the winning frontline customer service representative who on a daily basis provides quality service to customers.

Positive Attitude Is a Must Because Customer Service Is Difficult

One of the most difficult jobs in business is frontline customer service. These jobs

are also rewarding and offer challenges other noncustomer-contact jobs can't offer. The job is definitely not for the faint of heart; a certain tenacity is required.

Frontline service people are constantly faced with situations requiring the utmost skill to satisfy the customer. In this environment, establishing and maintaining a positive attitude is not the easiest of tasks. But it must be done, for frontline service without the touch and display of a positive attitude is marginal—at best.

The More Difficult the Job, the Stronger the Need for a Positive Attitude

A strong job performance correlates directly with the attitude of the person doing the job. This is especially true in customer service, where the toughest ego can be bruised and the spirits of the best can be dampened temporarily. The job is nearly always filled with adversity. On certain days, customer problems and other demands are enough to leave the service provider still talking about them late at night. Join a group of frontline service people for pizza after work or at a company picnic, and the conversation will always be about customers—problems and successes.

The customer service position absorbs the individual providing the service. For the right person, however, the personal satisfaction is great. One of the characteristics of this "right person" is a positive attitude.

How Frontline Service People Survive

Long-term frontline people survive by two means. First, they possess the necessary skills to satisfy needs. Second, they have a positive customer service attitude. Many came to their jobs with positive attitudes and strengthen them as they gain experience. Others developed an attitude that serves as a foundation for success. Either situation requires an occasional attitude renewal. This renewal is needed because no one can embrace or display a positive attitude at all times. Even the most positive person needs an activity that will serve to renew her attitude. Renewal comes in the form of internal reminders to ourselves simply to start thinking positive. We may need to get away. To exercise. To rest. To change our focus. In short, the successful customer service provider is wise enough to do what is required to get back on the positive-attitude track.

Attitude Is a Choice

If you tell someone with a bad attitude that he has selected his attitude, you will probably get an argument. Circumstances, experiences and maybe even childhood, they will proclaim, dictate the way we all think and act.

Yes, our attitude can be shaped by those factors, but it also is a matter of choice. Many argue that physical well-being is related to attitude. Interestingly, those with a positive attitude tend to believe the physical well-being theory, while those with less than a positive attitude tend to doubt it.

Elwood N. Chapman, in his excellent book *Attitude: Your Most Priceless Possession*, has this to say about the role of attitude:

> *In the work environment, as in your personal life, it is your attitude that makes the difference. Building and maintaining healthy relationships among superiors and co-workers is the key to success in any organization. Nothing contributes more to this process than a positive attitude. A positive attitude will expand your network. When positive, you transmit friendly signals.*

Customers, co-workers, and superiors are more open to you.

Attitude Is More Than Cute Sayings and Personality

The display of a positive attitude is not a technique or gimmick that can be drummed up for a particular moment. Nor is it centered around the utterance of phrases and sayings with positive overtones. Such sayings have their place, but serve only as reminders to be positive.

A positive attitude is deeply rooted in the character of the individual. However, even character aspects can be learned.

Developing and Maintaining a Positive Customer Service Attitude

The ten suggestions presented here will help customer service providers strengthen their attitude.

1. **Recognize Attitude as a Matter of Choice.** Select an attitude that is customer focused and one that sees the positive aspects and opportunities of customer situations.

2. **Strive to Improve your Attitude.** Continue to strive to improve your attitude. Don't accept negative thoughts, but instead find the positive course.

3. **Be Proactive with Customers.** Don't wait; act positively.

4. **Use Positive Language.** Especially with customers. State what you can do, not what you can't. Present information in positive terms.

5. **Avoid Negative Input.** Avoid those who offer negative thoughts and actions.

6. **Promote a Positive Attitude in Your Work Group.** Set an example for others to follow.

7. **Keep Your Self-Talk Positive.** Think positively of yourself, your abilities and your work. Adopt a positive view of the world.

8. **Listen to Your Attitude.** Hear what you say to customers.

9. **Remain Positive with High Expectations.** Don't become complacent.

10. **Carry Your Positive Attitude to All Phases of Your Life.** Reinforce your positive work attitude at home, and vice versa.

Conclusion

Attitude *is* a choice. We select a positive attitude and display it as a way to remain mentally healthy and to satisfy customers. Customers, like all of us, want to work with people who are positive. These attitudes come naturally for many, but can also be developed and learned. Attitude is a character issue, not a mere function of personality. However, personalities are definitely strengthened by a positive attitude. Individuals with positive attitudes are like magnets; others are drawn to them.

Case Study: The Positive Attitude Wins

This is a true story about an organization. The name is purposely withheld. It is a story of a sales unit consisting of customer service representatives (CSRs) who supported their internal customer, salespeople, and directly worked with customers on service issues and problems.

A Deteriorating Situation
The morale and attitude among the CSRs was poor. There was, for example, lots of drama within the group about organizational changes, new policies and especially an ongoing conflict with the salespeople. The CSRs felt like second-class citizens and thought the salespeople and sales management were too demanding. The relationship between the sales-support manager and the sales manager was rocky; this added to the problem. The sales-support manager and her CSRs often took a defiant stance. In short, the situation was negatively affecting everyone, including customers.

The Customer Gets Involved
Sixty percent of the organization's revenue came from just one account, a well-known multistate financial institution. This account required the full-time services of one account manager, two salespersons and four CSRs. Occasionally, when the activity was especially heavy, additional CSRs would be assigned. Sales-support and sales managers were personally involved with the account and well positioned with the decision makers. The relationship between the account and the organization had always been strong. They were mutually dependent on each other.

Surprise!
Unexpectedly, the key decision maker from the account asked for a private meeting with the account manager, sales manager and sales-support manager. The four met, and the decision maker conducted a short, to-the-point meeting. He expressed his overall dissatisfaction with the support he was getting from the organization. He cited numerous incidents where sales and sales support refused to cooperate, which caused problems. He talked about how upset some of his people had been with the organization. Finally, he pointed to the "attitude" of the entire organization. He bluntly said, "The attitude used to be, 'How can we help?' Now it is one of finger pointing, delays, confusion and ineptness."

The meeting ended with the sales and sales-support manager assuring the customer that everything would improve immediately.

Action Is Taken

A variety of activities designed to improve attitude and basic relationships between sales and sales support were put together. Meetings between the groups to define issues of concern and to promote teamwork were successful. A major improvement was the physical integration of the two units; sales and sales support had been in a separate office; now they were colocated in the same area. Most important, the sales and sales-support managers came to agreement on the issues and both realized they needed to take a more positive leadership role. Attitude and cooperation became a discussion topic in every meeting.

The Customer Is Asked

The customer was periodically asked, "How are we doing?" Over time, the feedback became more and more positive. This feedback was shared with all employees and often discussed in group meetings. The "Ask the Customer" program became standard operating procedure for the organization.

The Organization Was Fortunate

The organization was fortunate, its customer was bold enough to confront its employees regarding problems and attitude. As we discussed earlier, most customers tend not to complain, but instead quietly go away. The customer's directness, in this case, shocked the managers into action. Although much of their motivation for emphasizing cooperation and a positive attitude was fear of losing the account, they also were genuinely concerned about their failure to foster a positive customer service environment and attitude.

The Future of the Customer Service Job

Of all the changes the twenty-first century will bring, perhaps the most significant will be change itself—change that occurs often, faster and affects more people. Instead of one job with one organization, most people will experience multiple jobs and even multiple careers over the course of their working lives. This may require moving to various parts of the country in order to secure employment, working for oneself, enduring periods of unemployment, and retiring not at all or very late in life. Employers will demand the learning of new skills, as job needs and technology continually evolve. The economy we live and compete in has become less local or national and more global. Good jobs will be available, but they will require high skills. Competition for such jobs will be strong.

Skills, Skills and More Skills

One thing about the future is abundantly clear: Those with the highest education and skills will fare better than those who are unskilled or have marginal skills. Today, employee earnings are increasingly based on the skills of the individual rather than job classification. Organizations are downsizing, which means they have fewer employees and a correspondingly higher demand for employees with multiple skills. The old production worker who performed one repetitive task is rapidly disappearing.

Robert Reich, a former Harvard professor of economics and currently secretary of labor in the Clinton administration, has written an interesting book that all service providers and young Americans should read. In *The Work of Nations*, Reich describes aspects of the global economy. He depicts the economic fate of Americans in this manner: "No longer are Americans rising or falling together, as if in one large national boat. We are, increasingly, in different, smaller boats." He projects three broad work categories for America's future. He calls them "routine production services, in-person services and symbolic-analytic services." Reich describes the first two categories as closely supervised workers who perform repetitive tasks. He separates in-person service workers from production workers: "The big difference between in-person servers and routine producers is that services must be provided person to person and thus are not sold worldwide." The third category of future jobs Reich calls symbolic-analytic services. Jobs in this category "include all the problem solving, problem identifying and strategic brokering activities. . . ."

Where Does the Customer Service Job Fit?

If you accept Robert Reich's view of the future, you have to ask yourself, Where do I fit? What's my future? If we examine the three categories of jobs described and try to place the typical customer service representative, the logical location is the in-person service worker category. When the service response is restricted or limited to repetitive actions, then the low end of this category fits well. An example might be in a bank where a service provider at the new-accounts desk only opens new checking and savings accounts for walk-in customers.

At the other end of the service spectrum is the representative who identifies customer problems, solves them and follows up with the customer to ensure satisfaction. An example might be frontline service in a computer-software organization. The customer has a probem. Frontline helps define the problem and its cause and suggests alternatives or particular

services or products to resolve the customer's problem. This type of job extends across categories of the in-person services and reaches into problem-solving services (symbolic-analytic services). However, it probably rests mostly at the high end of the in-person services category. When contrasted with the "new accounts" bank service job, the software frontline service position requires considerably more education and skills. Obviously, the software employee has a brighter future and can demand a much higher salary.

Skills Will Determine Your Future

During America's post–World War II economic expansion and dominance, high-paying production jobs were plentiful. High school graduates routinely earned strong middle-class incomes while enjoying numerous fringe benefits, including retirement pay. As we all know, those days and the plentiful production jobs are gone, and there is no indication they will return. Today, routine production jobs are scattered around the world, and more Americans are employed in the service sector than in manufacturing. Other nations, with lower wages and few regulations, have often become the manufacturer's first choice.

The future is still full of opportunity, especially in the service category. But again, skills and education are required to succeed. In addition, a capacity to learn and be trained, well into adult life, will be a key to success for many. Trying to make a mid-life job or career change without the ability to be trained in new subjects and skills will be difficult, if not impossible.

What Can the Service Provider Do?

The skills that a service provider begins with today will not likely be enough to sustain the individual over the course of a service career. The individual must be able to grow and adapt to new environments, situations and customer demands. The ability to manage a conversation with a customer successfully will always be important. However, to move to the high end of the service job classifications and to remain there will require considerable education, skills and knowledge in a variety of important areas. Those areas include an ability to identify and solve problems, advanced product knowledge, an understanding of customer applications of products and services, knowledge of new technologies and how they apply to customers, increased knowledge of the customer's business, and a host of other areas of knowledge and skill.

Is the Future Scary or Challenging?

The theme of the chapter on a positive attitude was **choice**. How you perceive the future is also a choice. The higher your skills and education, the more opportunity you will see and the more you will feel challenged and excited to be participating.

Will it be easier than in the past? It is doubtful that many will find it easy to get ahead and have challenging careers. But success is attainable for those willing to work and continue to strive for improvement. One requirement will be more proactive behavior. Author Stephen R. Covey, in his book *The 7 Habits of Highly Effective People*, states, "Many people who end up with the good jobs are the proactive ones who are solutions to problems, not problems themselves, who seize the initiative to do whatever is necessary, consistent with correct principles, to get the job done."

In summary, the future is bright and full of opportunity. High skills and a strong education are a must. The choice is yours.

Acknowledgment

Special thanks to Linguatec, Inc.,
Sunnyvale, California. Linguatec, Inc.
provides communication skill training in
both language and inter-cultural communication for the multi-cultural workforce.

Bibliography

Albrecht, Karl. *The Only Thing That Matters*, Harper Business, a Division of Harper Collins Publishing, 1992.

Albrecht, Karl & Ron Zemke. *Service America*, Dow Jones-Irwin, 1985.

Anderson, Kristin & Ron Zemke. *Delivering Knock Your Socks Off Service*, American Management Association, 1991.

Carr, Clay. *Front-Line Customer Service*, John Wiley & Sons, 1990.

Chapman, Elwood N. *Attitude: Your Most Priceless Possession*, Crisp Publications, 1987.

Covey, Stephen R. *The 7 Habits of Highly Effective People*, Simon and Schuster, 1989.

Davidow, William H. & Bro Uttal. *Total Customer Service*, Harper & Rowe, 1989.

Desatnick, Robert L. *Managing to Keep the Customer*, Jossey-Bass Publishers, 1987.

Hanan, Mack & Peter Karp. *Customer Satisfaction*, American Management Association, 1991.

Hanan, Mack, James Cribbin & Jack Donis. *Systems Selling Strategies*, American Management Association, 1978.

Hinton, Thomas D. *The Spirit of Service*, Kendall/Hunt Publishing Co., 1991.

Kearney, Elizabeth I., Ph.D. & Michael J. Bandley, Ph.D., *Everyone Is a Customer*, Sterling Press, 1990.

Laborde, Genie Z. *Influencing With Integrity*, Syntony Publishing, 1983.

Lash, Linda M. *The Complete Guide to Customer Service*, John Wiley & Sons, 1989.

LeBoeuf, Michael, Ph.D. *The Greatest Management Principle in the World*, G. P. Putnam & Sons, 1985.

McKenna, Regis. *Relationship Marketing*, Addison-Wesley Publishing Co., 1991.

BIBLIOGRAPHY

Reich, Robert B. *The Work of Nations*, Alfred A. Knopf, 1991.

Rosander, A. C. *The Quest for Quality in Services*, American Society for Quality Control, 1989.

Silverman-Goldzimer, Linda. *I'm First*, Rawson Associates, 1989.

Zemke, Ron & Dick Schaaf. *The Service Edge*, New American Library, 1989.

Catalog

If you have enjoyed this book, you will
be pleased to learn that we specialize
in creative instructional books for both
individual and professional growth.

Call or write for our free catalog:

CRISP PUBLICATIONS, INC.
1200 Hamilton Court
Menlo Park, CA 94025

TEL. 1-800-442-7477
FAX: 1-415-323-5800